Conflict and Consensus in Switzerland

Conflict and
Consensus in
Switzerland ⊕

Carol L. Schmid

University of California Press
Berkeley • Los Angeles • London

University of California Press
Berkeley and Los Angeles, California
University of California Press, Ltd.
London, England
© 1981 by
The Regents of the University of California
Printed in the United States of America

1 2 3 4 5 6 7 8 9

Library of Congress Cataloging in Publication Data

Schmid, Carol L.
  Conflict and consensus in Switzerland.

  Bibliography: p. 183
  Includes index.
    1. Switzerland—Ethnic relations. 2. Pluralism—(Social
sciences) 3. Switzerland—Politics and government.
4. Minorities—Switzerland. 5. Religion and state—Switzerland.
6. Multilingualism—Switzerland. I. Title.
HN603.S35   305.8'009494   80-18458
ISBN 0-520-04079-1

To Peter, without whom this work would not have been

Contents

Preface

I first became interested in intergroup relations in Switzerland during a stay there in 1970-71. Having grown up in the more homogeneous American culture, I found it fascinating to live in the midst of four language communities. I was often struck by the orderly and matter-of-fact way in which cultural and linguistic differences were treated in this small multicultural society. My interest in questions of cultural coexistence and conflict was reawakened upon moving to another plurilingual society; but in Canada, matters of language and culture excited the temperaments and sentiments of both linguistic groups. Against this backdrop, I decided to seriously pursue the study of intergroup relations in Switzerland.

In the course of this study, I have become indebted to a great many people who have given me information and assistance. Dr. Heinz Ries, now professor at the University of Trier, and his wife, Marie-Louise, provided me with continual help and hospitality during my stay in Switzerland. Bruno Kehrli of the Centre suisse de documentation en matière d'enseignement et d'éducation aided me in construction of the sample design and in carrying out the questionnaire.

Numerous teachers and administrators in various parts of Switzerland allowed me to administer the questionnaire, and gave me valuable insights on Swiss education. Among these I would particularly like to thank Hans Joos, Robert Lüthy, Pierre Salamin, Jacques Sauter, Martin Sommer, and René Stöhr. Joseph Eigenmann, Werner Hadorn, Jacques Lefert, Alain Pichard, André Rieder, and Hans Utz also helped me in various capacities. Mrs. Madeleine Schmid-Stöhr provided hospitality and friendly living quarters. A Canada Council Doctoral Fellowship made much of my field work possible, and a Guilford College Research Fellowship helped defray the costs of preparing the manuscript.

I would also like to thank Howard Brotz and Kenneth McRae for their continual help throughout the course of this work, as well as Cyrus Johnson, Val Lorwin, Jürg Siegenthaler, and Jürg Steiner for reading portions of the manuscript. Finally, I want to express my appreciation to Doris Boylan and Olive Jenkins for painstakingly typing the book, and to Christian Schmid for production of the questionnaire.

C.L.S.

1| The Swiss Enigma

To many outside observers, it has long been a major enigma of politics that, in an age of cultural nationalism, Switzerland has managed to weld four different language groups and two major religions into a stable and relatively amicable confederation of cantons. Writing in the mid 1960s, Etzioni (1965: 22, 35) mentioned Canada, the Union of South Africa, Switzerland, Belgium, Nigeria, and India as instances of national communities without a shared culture that enjoyed relatively high levels of political integration. Of these six multicultural societies, today only Switzerland can still serve as a convincing example of a fragmented culture whose overall political unity is not threatened.

This study will examine how Switzerland manages its ethnic diversity, as well as some of the problems now facing this small multicultural society. Intergroup relations in Switzerland have largely escaped the attention of students cf ethnic relations. The paucity of literature appears to be related to an overemphasis on conflict and discord, often at the expense of those factors associated with cultural coexistence. Such selectivity has created a prevailing pessimism about the prospects for democracy in severely divided plural societies. Williams (1977) observes that the total spectrum of ethnic outcomes must be analyzed; peaceful processes of accommodation are no less worthy of attention than civil turmoil.

Sometimes Swiss coexistence is attributed to the fortunate accidents of history and geography, but no serious inquirer can be content with an explanation so simple and at the same time so unhelpful. Rather, these claims of Swiss "exceptionalism"[1] have

1. This view is expressed in such titles and subtitles as "Der Sonderfall der

1

tended to conceal important elements of public policy as well as common problems faced by other multi-ethnic societies.

Some Historical Background on the Status of Swiss Linguistic and Religious Minorities

"There seems," writes McRae (1964:5), "to be a widespread impression that the current happy condition of linguistic equality in Switzerland has its roots deep in Swiss history." At best, this explanation is only partially true. The cultural and linguistic variety of Switzerland is something comparatively recent. The first five centuries of the Confederation as well as the fundamental tradition of Switzerland belong to the German-speaking population. Of the thirteen cantons[2] admitted into the Confederation before the Reformation, only Fribourg had any significant French-speaking population, and during this time it was ruled by an urban aristocracy which made repeated efforts to Germanize it.

From the sixteenth century onward, French-, Italian-, and Romansch-speaking populations were associated in various ways with the Confederation. The League of the Grisons, Valais, Neuchâtel, and the ecclesiastical principality of Basel (which became the Jura district of Bern) were associated as allies of the Confederates. Ticino and Vaud, as well as part of present-day German Switzerland (including the present-day canton of Thurgau and much of Aargau), were ruled as subject territories by one or several cantons. These allies and subject territories did not obtain equality with the thirteen cantons of the Old Regime until much later. However, a strong heritage of communal independence which can be traced back to the beginnings of Switzerland helped to mediate a tendency to dominate the minority language groups by the ruling cantons (Meyer, 1952:358-360). This respect for local autonomy and linguistic diversity was an important factor in

---

Schweiz" in Deutsch (1976), *Die Schweiz als ein paradigmatischer Fall politischer Integration*, and *Die Schweiz als Antithese* by Lüthy (1969: esp. 10-12). The paucity of literature on intergroup relations in Switzerland has also been exacerbated by some Swiss authors who, enamored by the "uniqueness" of the national experience, have tended to take an insular view of Swiss politics and interethnic relations; as well as by some comparative scholars who, lacking a thorough understanding of the Swiss case, have neatly pigeonholed it as "deviant." See, for example, de Salis, *La Suisse diverse et paradoxale* (1971), and Rabuska and Shepsle, *Politics in Plural Societies: A Theory of Democratic Instability* (1972:208-212).

2. The thirteen cantons were Zurich, Bern, Lucerne, Uri, Schwyz, Unterwalden, Glarus, Zug, Basel, Fribourg, Solothurn, Schaffhausen, and Appenzell.

attracting the allegiance of the subordinate areas—which, when they had the option, decided to remain with their overseers and protectors.

Invasion by the French army in 1798 spelled an end to the ancient Confederation of thirteen cantons. This network of feudal obligations and aristocratic privileges could not be maintained under the impact of the ideas of the French Revolution. It was replaced by the Helvetic Republic, whose constitution was based on the conceptions of the Enlightenment and the rights of man. Embodying the French tradition of centralization and authoritarian executive power, the new regime found support only in a few areas like Vaud and Aargau, which were enjoying their newly acquired independence. Despite opposition, it transformed Switzerland almost overnight into a modern state. The 1798 Constitution abolished all privileges and established the equality of individuals and of territories. For the first time, it also created a common Swiss nationality with a parliament representing the whole country (Bonjour, 1938:323).

In addition, it had important consequences for the relationship between the language groups, as many authors (Kohn, 1956:47; McRae, 1964:6) have pointed out. As Bonjour (1952:230) notes:

> . . . By raising the French and Italian subject districts to the status of cantons with equal rights, the Helvetic Republic founded a multilingual Switzerland. In this way it checked the growth of a different language for rulers and ruled wherever there were signs of it. . . . Helvetic laws and resolutions were printed in German and French and in Italian if required. In this way a new application was given to the principle of equality before the law which was to illuminate the future and help to solve the problem of nationality.

The spiritual leaders of the Helvetic Republic were sufficiently inventive to draw up a plan patterned on existing conditions rather than on unity of language, which had previously been considered the deciding national characteristic. When it was possible to make German-, French-, and Italian-speaking people into one nation, the point had been reached at which "the barbaric prejudices broke down, which make men rivals, then enemies, and finally slaves," and a greater, truly European unity was produced in which "there was a marriage of German profundity with French elegance and Italian taste," declared La Harpe, a native of Vaud and one of the framers of the Helvetic Constitution. The ultimate goal was to overcome the differences which divide men, until all nations become one (Weilenmann, 1925:288).

Despite its benefits to the linguistic minorities, the Helvetic Republic conflicted too strongly with the entrenched sentiments of local autonomy and of traditional diversity. The citizenry revolted against uniformity, and widespread unrest rendered the constitution unworkable. In 1803 Napoleon intervened and imposed his Mediation, which restored to each canton its own government. The new Constitution of 1803, which was intended to keep Switzerland in a state of weakness and dependence on France, was, however, more in harmony with the country's mood than that of the Helvetic Republic (Bohnenblust, 1974:380-381). It maintained the chief gains of the Helvetic period: old subject districts and the tangled network of ancient privileges were abolished, and intercantonal or foreign alliances were prohibited. The linguistic equality of 1798 was also maintained, with the inclusion of the cantons of Ticino and Vaud. The other subject German-speaking territories of Aargau and Thurgau, and the associated lands of Grisons and St. Gallen, were admitted as cantons with equal rights, bringing the total of sovereign cantons to nineteen. Despite the harsh demands of Swiss troops in Napoleonic service, the Mediation period secured ten years of well-being and order for the nation at a time when most European lands suffered from wars and revolutions. The 1803 Constitution remained a source of inspiration for the Swiss liberals in the troubled decades after 1815.

After Napoleon's downfall, the cantons resumed most of their old authority and reverted to German as the official language. On the verge of civil war, it was only under the influence of the Allied powers that Switzerland reached an understanding on a new constitution in 1815. Under the new Federal Pact, Switzerland became once more a confederation of sovereign states united for only two purposes: common defense and the maintenance of internal order. The Congress of Vienna had allowed the return to Switzerland of its ancient allies Valais, Neuchâtel, and Geneva, which now took their place as independent cantons. With the addition of these territories, Switzerland assumed the basic boundaries it has today.

Through the extension of civil rights initiated by the revolutions, language differences gained in political importance in Switzerland. This was especially the case when the followers of the progressive and conservative parties did not belong to the same language group. In the canton of Bern, the French and Catholic districts of the Jura attempted to break away from the old German-speaking Protestant canton; in Fribourg, the German and Protestant district of Murten defended itself against the French and Catholic majority of the canton; in Catholic Valais, a civil war broke out between the German-speaking groups of the upper Valais and the more liberal French-speaking groups in lower Valais (Weilenmann, 1925:207-208).

Religious bitterness, which had temporarily died down, also reappeared. The division between Catholic and Reformed has been a moving force in Swiss history since the Reformation. Religious differences, even in those instances where religious and linguistic boundaries reinforced each other, have always been more salient than linguistic ones in Switzerland.

The Reformation split Switzerland into two opposing camps. From the first religious battle in 1529 until the nineteenth century, the division between the two faiths was clear and remained unchanged. The present-day cantons of Uri, Schwyz, Unterwalden (both halves), Lucerne, Zug, Fribourg, Solothurn, Ticino, and Valais, as well as Appenzell Inner Rhoden and Jura, remained Catholic, while Zurich, Bern, both Basels, Schaffhausen, Appenzell Outer Rhoden, Vaud, Neuchâtel, and Geneva adhered predominantly to the Protestant faith. In Glarus, St. Gallen, Grisons, Aargau, and Thurgau the two faiths co-existed. The religious division was influential in shaping the *Weltanschauung* of the ordinary citizen. A person was born into either a Protestant canton or a Catholic one. Conversions were rare. Most of the Catholic cantons had declared Roman Catholicism to be the state religion. Some would not even allow Protestants to settle. In mixed cantons, hostility between the two faiths was also a salient feature of the political and social landscape. Liberty of conscience did not exist in either Protestant or Catholic cantons. Even under the Act of Mediation, in which most of the rights of man were insured, the constitution did not guarantee freedom of religion or freedom of conscience. A change of religion or marriage with a person of a different faith could be punished by withdrawing citizenship (Bohnenblust, 1974:382).

Switzerland after 1815 was a collection of small states jealously guarding their sovereignty, not very different from what it had been before Napoleonic times. "Democracy," de Tocqueville observed in the 1830s, "was less a regular form of government than a weapon habitually used to destroy, and sometimes to defend, the old society" (1969 ed.:737). In 1788 Alexander Hamilton and James Madison cited the example of the Swiss Federation in *The Federalist* as a warning of the dangers of weak government. "Whatever efficacy the union may have had in ordinary cases," they wrote, "it appears that the moment a cause of difference sprang up, capable of trying its strength, it failed" (1941 ed.:119). This discord rose with the revival of the spirit of the French Revolution in the Switzerland of the 1830s; and in 1832 the seven leading "regenerated" cantons—Zurich, Bern, Lucerne, Solothurn, St. Gallen, Aargau, and Thurgau—united to protect their new constitutions and to press for a revision of the 1815 Pact along more liberal lines.

Spearheaded by the decision of the Confederation not to enforce Article 12 of the Federal Pact (which guaranteed the maintenance of religious orders in the cantons) against the canton of Aargau, which had suppressed the operation of several monasteries, seven Catholic cantons—Lucerne, Uri, Schwyz, Unterwalden, Zug, Fribourg, and Valais—formed the Sonderbund (or separatist confederation) in 1845. This conflict was aggravated by religious and economic differences as well as by memories of former religious battles. The cantons of the Sonderbund were Catholic, rural, and conservative; they feared the prevailing liberalism of the Protestant cantons and the drive toward Swiss unification, which they saw as a threat to their religious and political traditions.

By 1847 the Radicals had a majority in the Diet and demanded that the Sonderbund be dissolved, because it was incompatible with the Federal Pact. When the Catholic cantons refused to acquiesce, the Diet ordered the dissolution by force of arms and appointed a moderate, Henri Dufour from Geneva, as commander-in-chief. The war was short-lived. The Catholic cantons were defeated in 25 days with a loss of only 128 men on both sides. Dufour helped to moderate the outcome of the war by repeated appeals to his troops to spare the opponents' civil population. In his proclamation, he stressed the fact that Catholic soldiers from Solothurn, Ticino, and St. Gallen were fighting in his army, while the general commanding the Sonderbund forces was a Protestant.

De Tocqueville (1969:736-737) was able to say in 1848 of the short-lived civil war that:

> Nowhere else has the democratic revolution . . . taken place in such strange and complicated circumstances. One people, composed of several races, speaking several languages, with several religious beliefs, various dissident sects, (and) two churches both equally established and privileged, (with) all political questions quickly turning into religious ones, and all religious questions ending up as political ones, (in short) two societies, one very old and the other very young, joined in marriage in spite of the age difference. That is a fair sketch of Switzerland (today).

The victors in the Swiss civil war were free to lay the foundation for the new nation. Although it was in their power to impose upon Switzerland a centralized authority, disregarding the need of the religious and linguistic minorities, they chose instead to compromise between the excessive federalism of the old regime and the complete unity advocated by the more extreme Radicals. Although it underwent a thorough revision in 1874, the 1848 Constitution in its basic aspects remains the constitution of Switzerland today.

The 1848 Constitution established a Council of States (or *Ständerat*) on the model of the old Diet and of the United States Senate, each canton being represented by two deputies. This Council allowed the linguistic and religious minorities—taken together—to have a blocking vote in federal legislation. In the National Council (or *Nationalrat*, patterned after the American House of Representatives), on the other hand, each canton is represented by delegates in proportion to its population. The 1848 Constitution guaranteed the complete equality of languages by declaring that German, French, and Italian are the national languages of Switzerland. In addition, freedom of worship was secured.

Our brief examination of Swiss history warns against accepting too literally an interpretation of Swiss harmony based primarily on fortunate accidents of history. The so-called "fortunate accidents" have often been more attributable to public policy and statesmanlike responsibility than to sheer luck. But on balance, there are a number of "accidental" and human factors that have shaped the current situation of intergroup relations in Switzerland. It is one of the fortunate accidents of Swiss history that the linguistic and religious boundaries do not coincide. Language conflict was moderated, since both religions had their adherents in every language area. Another fortunate circumstance that has tempered relations between linguistic groups is the fact that the smaller language groups were never forced to struggle for their rights. Rather, linguistic equality was imposed upon the old Confederation under the inspiration of the French Revolution. It should be pointed out, however, that there was by and large a heritage of fair language dealings prior to the Helvetic Republic; and that in a less conducive setting, linguistic equality imposed by a conquering force might later have had detrimental effects, when the alien power was no longer present. Responsible leadership has also played an important role in the success of the Swiss state. Finally, the more-than-fair treatment and overrepresentation of minorities in public life is another noteworthy factor influencing cultural coexistence in Switzerland.

Geography and the small size of the Swiss state have also been mentioned as factors contributing to Swiss exceptionalism. To what degree is cultural coexistence connected to the special geographical setting of Switzerland and the state's small population and limited power? Are these critical variables for the maintenance of ethnic harmony?

Considerations of Geography and the Smallness of the Swiss State

Switzerland is split into separate divisions not only by the main chain of the Alps, but also by the mountain ranges which extend outward from both sides of the Alps. Nature has hindered movement and exchange within the country more than with the neighboring countries of the same language group. Following the rivers from the heights of the Alps, it is possible to go almost unhindered northward through the same language region to the North Sea, southward to the Mediterranean, and westward to the Atlantic Ocean. In contrast, the inhabitants of the next Swiss village may speak a different language and have different customs and institutions.

Perhaps because of this lack of cohesion and their isolation, the Swiss territories lacked political unity until the fourteenth century. Neither the Habsburgs nor the Savoy or Milan dynasties succeeded in extending their domination to the whole country. Around the middle of the fourteenth century, the peasant communities of early Switzerland—Uri, Schwyz, and Unterwalden— which at the end of the thirteenth century agreed upon a common foreign policy, succeeded in forming an "eternal" Federation with the three towns at the approaches to the Alps: Lucerne, Zurich, and Bern. In the struggle against the Habsburgs, this league developed into the Confederation of the 8 Cantons through the addition of the mountain peasants of Glarus and the urban and rural inhabitants of Zug. In the second half of the fifteenth century the towns of Fribourg and Solothurn were admitted, and by 1513 the towns of Basel and Schaffhausen, as well as the mountainous territory of Appenzell, were included. This Confederation of the 13 Cantons formed the basis of Switzerland as a state, until the invasion of the French army in 1798.

Therefore the existence of Switzerland cannot be explained by reference to the power of a princely state, or to a safe geographical frontier, or to one language. The only state-building forces were those organizations developed in the Middle Ages by the people themselves. The inhabitants of the towns and alpine communities had the same interests: the safeguarding of the economy and internal peace, the achievement of self-government in the struggle against temporal and ecclesiastic nobility, and opposition to the growing territorial states. These common interests were strong enough to overcome the geographical, political, and ethnic divisions in the course of 200 years (Weilenmann, 1925).

In general, small states are less burdened by foreign policy and power considerations than larger states. Lorwin (1974:43) has observed that in this way size has helped to maintain the viability of the smaller European democracies of Belgium, Switzerland, Austria, and Holland. "Not being possessed, in the age of industrialism, of the means of international aggression, none of them has cherished illusions about its international role. . . . The Swiss cantons ceased to be expansionist when, with the Reformation, the existence of religious differences was accepted." This sort of realism had the further effect of making Switzerland more receptive to the admission of Socialist and Catholic parties, which in the larger states of Germany and France offended the hypernationalism of political leaders and powerful domestic groups.

Falke (1915:25) contends that the strong sense of moral obligation to the principle of neutrality, together with the smallness of the Swiss state, has conditioned national life and remolded the soul of the Swiss people.

> It makes a tremendous difference whether a man has been brought up to the thought: "You belong to a great power which one day must fight for world supremacy" or whether he must always say to himself: "If it should come finally to fighting, we can hope for nothing better than to keep what we already have." The two fundamentally different conceptions of life, in the light of which all detailed questions of existence take on a different appearance, much deeper than one is accustomed to assume, is the influence of the politics of a people upon its ethical attitude, and in the latter is influenced by the former. In this mutual action and reaction, the character of a people is formed.

By recognizing the limits to expansionism, small states may more easily accept solidarity in diversity. If this generalization holds true, the case of Switzerland should be of particular interest to multi-ethnic third-world states which, like Switzerland, are small in international power and geographical size.

Another factor which can foster solidarity is the external demands which are made on the system. In part, Swiss civic cohesion has been a negative process, facilitated by the inhabitants' universal fear of absorption by Austria, Germany, or France. However, the historic experience varies among nations, and from period to period, and sometimes from issue to issue in the same nation. In modern Switzerland, World War I exacerbated linguistic conflict, while the Nazi threat led to a reinforcement of the sense of national unity. Therefore, while the smallness of the state and external threats suggest factors which may aid national integration, by themselves they seem insufficient to promote cultural coexistence.

Cross-Cutting Cleavages

Another explanation often invoked to explain the stability and cohesion of the Swiss polity rests on the hypothesis that cross-cutting cleavages such as religion, language, etc., tend to create cross-pressures among the population which serve to moderate the intensity of political conflict. One of the difficulties of this hypothesis is that it has become so popular and so frequently used in such a wide variety of circumstances that it is in danger of losing much of its explanatory power.[3] Despite this and other difficulties, it currently represents one of the dominant views of Swiss society held by social and political scientists.[4]

Authors who utilize the cross-cutting hypothesis too often treat the divisions in society as static properties. For example, Steiner, in his book *Amicable Agreement Versus Majority Rule* (1974), attempts to explain in terms of 16 hypotheses how inter-subcultural hostility is moderated in Switzerland. These descriptive propositions are, however, explicitly linked to a specific period, the 1960s and early 1970s—a time when most ideological and political divisions had lost their previous salience. Thus at times Steiner's argument appears to be circular—he explains Switzerland's ability to regulate its "inter-subcultural hostility" by referring essentially to descriptions of that present happy state. Nordlinger (1972:15) makes a similar criticism of Steiner when he notes:

> The author claims to be explaining that society's [Switzerland's] success in regulating its intense religious and linguistic conflicts. Yet,

3. This hypothesis has been invoked by writers seeking to explain exactly opposite phenomena. For example, cross-cutting cleavages are said to account for the instability of the Third and Fourth Republics (Thompson, 1958:38), and for the stability of the Helvetic Confederation (Siegfried, 1956:57-58).

4. The cross-cutting hypothesis has been used as the main, or at least partial, explanation of Swiss cultural coexistence by many Swiss authors; see, for example, Mayer (1952 and 1968) and Steiner (1974).

the linguistic conflict never became intense, religious conflict was regulated in the nineteenth century, and [Steiner] deals almost exclusively with contemporary Swiss social and political patterns.

Steiner (1974:255) basically accepts the cross-cutting hypothesis, concluding that "there is usually a cross-cutting rather than a *verzuiling* (cumulative segmentation) between political parties, economic interest groups, voluntary associations, and newspapers."[5] His position seems to be that Swiss society is characterized by a set of multiple, cross-cutting political cleavages, of which none is so dominant as to exclude the influence of the others on the political process. While this assessment of Swiss society is probably currently correct, it has not always been the case. McRae (1975), for example, in an insightful paper, observes that Switzerland between the World Wars was sharply segmented along party and ideological lines, and that the well-balanced pressures which exist today (and about which Steiner writes) are a recent phenomenon. By failing to take into consideration the changing hierarchy of cleavages and their successive replacement over time, Steiner is in danger of ignoring the regulatory processes previously responsible for the depoliticalization or *ontzuiling* of the cleavage structures which are important contributing factors to the current moderation of inter-subcultural hostility.

Myths and Realities of the Swiss Case

In a distinguished lecture series entitled "History and Social Change: Some Myths and Realities," Rocher (1976) has elaborated three groups of factors which have influenced the patterns of history and social change. The first group of factors is attached to man and human action. The second group, which he observes is "usually put first," is a series of determinisms or constraints. Among these are demographic limitations such as the composition of the population according to language, religion, etc., and the size and natural landscape of the state. Finally, there is "sheer good, or bad luck, chance, coincidence, that also enter into the fabric of history, under the form of some accidental events or circumstances that bring together specific conditions favorable or unfavorable to the orientation of history in one direction rather than another one" (Rocher, 1976:10-12).

5. According to Steiner (1974:225), the one exception to cross-cutting "exists with the trade unions, which show a strong *verzuiling* with different political parties."

If we analyze the case of Switzerland in terms of these three factors, we find that most attempts to explain Swiss cultural coexistence have relied almost exclusively on the last two, largely neglecting the role of man and human action. This tendency, according to Rocher (1976:11), is apparent in the social sciences as a whole, which often emphasize some general laws at the expense of various human factors.

Consociational Democracy and the Swiss Experience

A recent challenge to this tendency is seen in the model of consociational democracy: basically, the role of the elite is seen as a critical factor in promoting the political stability of countries that have been characterized by substantial cultural fragmentation. The consociational model was developed in the late 1960s as an attempt to elaborate and extend Almond's classification of Western-style democratic regimes. Almond's typology contrasted stable two-party systems based on alternating majority governments, as exemplified by the "Anglo-American type," with the more volatile "continental European type" which is characterized by multi-party systems based on fluctuating ministerial coalitions (Almond, 1946:391-406). When it was observed that the political behavior of the smaller European countries did not fit either of these categories, there was a tendency to dismiss them as deviant cases, or as an intermediate category combining characteristics of the two.

The consociational model was, then, a response to the limited ability of earlier pluralist theory to explain the segmented but nevertheless stable smaller European countries: the Netherlands, Belgium, Austria, and Switzerland. The accommodationist patterns and processes connected with these countries have been termed by various authors as "consociational democracy" (Lijphart, 1968, 1969, 1977a; Daalder, 1974a and b), "segmented pluralism" (Lorwin, 1974), "concordant democracy (or *Konkordanzdemokratie*)" (Lehmbruch, 1968; Niemetz, 1970), and "proportional democracy (or *Proporzdemokratie*)" (Lehmbruch, 1967; Steiner, 1971).

Lijphart, who first coined the term "consociational democracy," is perhaps the most widely known among consociational theorists. Lijphart (1968:21) attributes a vital importance to the capacity and good will of the elites: "The essential characteristic of consociational democracy is not so much any particular institutional arrangement as overarching cooperation at the elite level with the deliberate aim of counteracting disintegrative tendencies in the system." Implicit in his reasoning is the assumption that only deliberate joint effort by the elites can stabilize the sharp cleavages in the system. He gives four requirements which must be fulfilled if consociational democracy is to be successful. First, the elites must be able to recognize the dangers of fragmentation; second, they must have some commitment to maintaining the system; third, they must be able to transcend subcultural cleavages at the elite level so that they are capable of working with the elites of the other subcultures; and finally, they must have the ability to forge appropriate solutions to accommodate the demands of divergent interests of the subcultures (Lijphart, 1968:22-23).

Beyond these prerequisites, Lijphart (1968:25-30) also identifies a number of characteristics of social structure and political culture which are conducive to the establishment or maintenance of consociational politics among elites in a fragmented system. He singles out the following factors: the existence of external threats to the country; a relatively low total load on the system as a whole; a popular acceptance of government by elite cartel; distinct lines of cleavage; and a balance of power among the subcultures.

The model of consociational democracy, when applied to the Swiss case, leaves many issues unsolved. By emphasizing the conscious and deliberate efforts of autonomous elite politics, it presupposes that popular sentiment and opinion play a negligible role in sustaining harmonious interethnic relations. This is at least a questionable proposition. Second, one wonders if the conditions of subcultural segmentation stipulated in the consociational model really hold today for the Swiss case. Consociational theorists have generally neglected to differentiate between cultural diversity and subcultural segmentation. As Daalder (1974a:615) points out: "Demographic variables are often assumed to be of attitudinal importance, with little investigation of the degree to which this is actually true." Thus, to obtain any real sense of how Switzerland manages its ethnic diversity, one must look at values and attitudes of the different cultural groups, as well as the political and social underpinnings of Swiss pluralism. Lüthy (1962:23), a well-known Swiss historian, writes:

> Good family portraits are never painted by members of the family concerned, and it would take a non-Swiss to produce a really good portrait of Switzerland. Usually the members of a given family are conscious of being individuals with marked physical and mental differences, and they are not necessarily very fond of each other. Only to the outsider do they appear to have the same nose or the same style of behavior—that is, a "family air."

The following chapters will sketch a portrait of Switzerland and the factors that have influenced intergroup relations in this small multicultural society. Viewing the Swiss panorama of ethnic relations from the vantage point of the United States, my picture of Switzerland will likely be different from that painted by a family member. "A stranger," de Tocqueville (1969:20) observed, "often hears important truths at his host's fireside, truths which he might not divulge to his friends."

2| The Ethnic Factor:

Foundations of a Multicultural Society

Several authors have pointed out that Switzerland provides a striking example of a case where "numerical minorities" are not synonymous with "sociological minorites."[1]

> For several centuries the French and Italian Swiss have not been minorities in our [sociological] sense of the term, nor have they given up lingual and cultural differences from the German Swiss, who make up three-fourths of the population. (Simpson and Yinger, 1965:22)

> No effort whatsoever is made by the Swiss Germans, who are in the overwhelming majority numerically, to assert any linguistic dominance. There are no linguistic minorities, either in a legal or in an informal sense. (Mayer, 1951:162)

> The attitude of the Swiss to their religious differences is much the same as their attitude to their language differences. After a long rivalry which once attained a degree of passionate violence difficult to imagine today, religious peace prevailed. And now there is not a single Swiss who imagines the national unity could be furthered by any particular confessional preference. (Siegfried, 1956:50)

What are the foundations for linguistic and religious coexistence? What disadvantages do the minorities face? Are there mechanisms in Swiss society that help to compensate for their numeri-

---

1. Probably the most frequently cited sociological definition in the area of minority group studies is that of Louis Wirth (1945:347). He defines a minority as "a group of people who, because of their physical or cultural characteristics, are singled out from others in the society in which they live for differential and unequal treatment and who therefore regard themselves as objects of collective discrimination."

cal weakness? These are the questions which will be addressed in this chapter. First we shall turn our attention to the composition and demographic characteristics of the Swiss population.

Linguistic and Religious Composition

Switzerland combines great linguistic and religious diversity in one small area. Its 6.3 million inhabitants—according to the 1970 census—speak four languages, as well as several dialects, and are divided into two major religions and several minor religious sects. In 1970 some 74 percent of Swiss citizens were German-speaking, 20 percent were French-speaking, 4 percent were Italian-speaking, and 1 percent spoke Romansch, a minor language spoken in a few Alpine valleys in the canton of Grisons. Since the Reformation, the Swiss citizenry has been fairly evenly divided along religious lines: 55 percent are Protestant and 43 percent Roman Catholic (*Annuaire Statistique de la Suisse*, 1976:28,30). Figures 1 and 2 show the geographic distribution of these linguistic and religious groups.

Focusing first on the linguistic diversity, we find that the proportion of Swiss citizens speaking the four languages has not changed significantly in recent decades (see Table 1). At most, we can discern a slight increase in the number of German-speaking Swiss citizens, resulting from the fact that the birthrate is higher in the German-speaking cantons, particularly the Catholic ones. Although the difference in fertility might at first glance be expected to disturb the linguistic balance, it is offset by two compensating factors. First, the difference in fertility between the French- and German-speaking areas of the country has been partly mitigated by the relatively high birthrate in the predominantly French-speaking Catholic cantons of Fribourg and Valais. Second, and more noteworthy, are the differences in internal migration. The French regions of the country have proved much more attractive to German-speaking migrants than the German regions have to French-speaking Swiss. Furthermore, the German Swiss migrants tend to become rapidly assimilated. By comparison, the few French Swiss who move into the German-speaking part of Switzerland seem to take much longer to assimilate (Mayer, 1952:167-70; Siegfried, 1956:75).[2]

2. As an example, I met a French Swiss family whose son, after living in Zurich most of his life, returned to French Switzerland to attend university. The parents also returned to French Switzerland after retirement. Other families I encountered had retained French as their family language after three or more

TABLE 1. Percentage of Swiss citizens by mother tongue
(figures for total resident population, including foreigners,
in parentheses)

Census	German	French	Italian	Romansch
1880	— (71.3%)	— (21.4%)	— (5.7%)	— (1.4%)
1910	72.7% (69.1)	22.1% (21.1)	3.9% (8.1)	1.2% (1.1)
1930	73.7 (71.9)	21.0 (20.4)	4.0 (6.0)	1.2 (1.1)
1950	74.1 (72.1)	20.6 (20.3)	4.0 (5.9)	1.1 (1.0)
1960	74.4 (69.3)	20.2 (18.9)	4.1 (9.5)	1.0 (0.9)
1970	74.5 (64.9)	20.1 (18.1)	4.0 (11.9)	1.0 (0.8)

Source: *Annuaire Statistique de la Suisse* (1976:28).

TABLE 2. Percentage of Swiss citizens by religion
(with figures for total resident population, including foreigners,
in parentheses)

Census	Protestant	Catholic	Jew	Others
1880	— (58.5%)	— (40.8%)	— (0.3%)	— (0.4%)
1910	61.4% (56.1)	37.8% (42.5)	0.2% (0.5)	0.6% (0.9)
1930	60.0 (57.3)	38.6 (41.0)	0.3 (0.4)	1.1 (1.3)
1950	58.5 (56.3)	40.3 (42.2)	0.2 (0.4)	1.0 (1.1)
1960	57.1 (52.7)	41.9 (45.9)	0.2 (0.4)	0.8 (1.0)
1970	55.0 (47.8)	43.4 (49.7)	0.2 (0.3)	1.4 (2.2)

Source: *Annuaire Statistique de la Suisse* (1976:30).

As with language, there has also existed a religious equilibrium
for many years, as shown in Table 2. The proportion of Catholics
among Swiss citizens has increased slightly since 1910, partly as a
result of the naturalization of Catholic aliens, of whom 70-80,000
were granted Swiss citizenship between 1910 and 1930, but mostly
as a result of fertility differentials between Catholics and Protestants (Mayer, 1952:180-181). On the other hand, if we consider
the entire population of Switzerland, including resident foreigners, we find that the increase in the Catholic population is much
more dramatic. This is due mainly to the large number of foreign
workers, primarily from Italy, who adhere to the Catholic faith.

---

generations in German Switzerland. A large French church in Zurich (known
locally as the *französische Kirche*) helps to unite the Protestant, French-speaking
community.

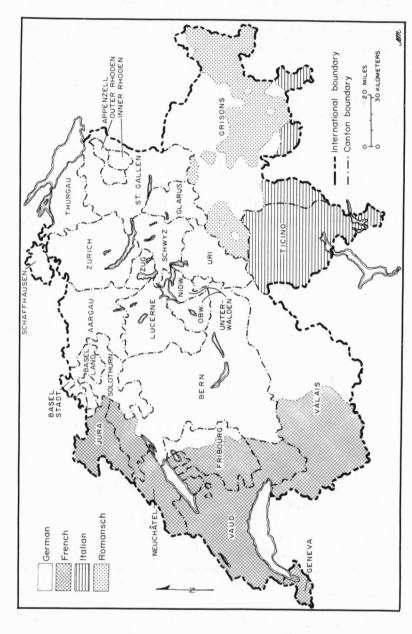

Figure 1. Geographic distribution of language groups in Switzerland.

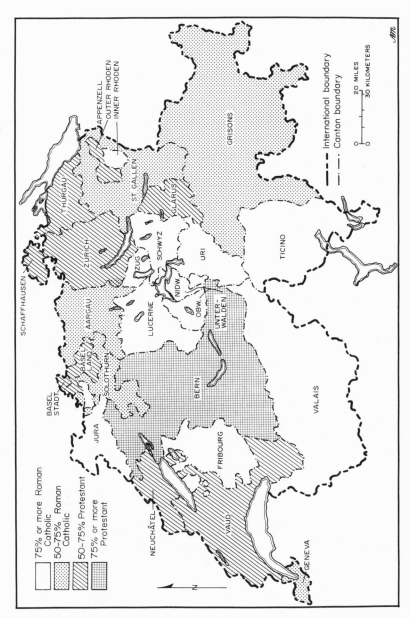

Figure 2. Geographic distribution of religious groups in Switzerland.

75% or more Roman
Catholic

50–75% Roman
Catholic

50–75% Protestant

75% or more
Protestant

International boundary
Canton boundary

20 MILES
30 KILOMETERS

SCHAFFHAUSEN

THURGAU

APPENZELL
OUTER RHODEN
INNER RHODEN

ST. GALLEN

GRISONS

ZURICH

GLARUS

ZUG

SCHWYZ

URI

TICINO

BASEL
STADT

AARGAU

LUCERNE

NIDW.

OBW.
UNTER-
WALDEN

BASEL
LAND

SOLOTHURN

JURA

BERN

VALAIS

FRIBOURG

NEUCHÂTEL

VAUD

GENEVA

N

This movement has also increased the population of Italian speakers present in Switzerland.

Taken together, the linguistic and religious components provide a mosaic of great complexity. It is one of those "fortunate accidents" of Swiss history that the linguistic and religious boundaries do not coincide, but often serve to offset one another. Thus there are Protestant majorities in two French-speaking cantons: Vaud with 61 percent, and Neuchâtel with 58 percent. Geneva is divided between the two faiths, and Valais and Fribourg, the two bilingual cantons with French-speaking majorities, along with the newly-formed canton of Jura, are strongly Catholic. German Switzerland also reflects a great diversity of religion. Nine German-speaking cantons or half-cantons are predominantly Catholic, and seven cantons or half-cantons have Protestant majorities, with Aargau split almost exactly between the two faiths. Ticino, the only Italian-speaking canton, is overwhelmingly Catholic, but the Romansch-speakers of the Grisons, like the French and German-speaking Swiss, are divided into Protestant and Catholic areas (see Table 3).

Federalism and the Ethnic Factor

One of the most important characteristics of the Swiss linguistic and religious pattern is its close link with federalism. Switzerland is a federation of 26 cantons and half-cantons which are sovereign in all matters except those expressly delegated to the federal government. The great majority of the cantons are officially unilingual. Therefore, although Switzerland maintains more than one official language, the languages are spoken in clearly defined territorial areas. The cantons of Geneva, Vaud, Neuchâtel, and Jura are French-speaking; Ticino is Italian-speaking; and the cantons of Zurich, Lucerne, Uri, Schwyz, Unterwalden (composed of two half-cantons: Obwalden and Nidwalden), Glarus, Zug, Solothurn, Basel (which is divided into Basel-Stadt and Basel-Land), Schaffhausen, Appenzell (which consists of Appenzell Inner Rhoden and Appenzell Outer Rhoden), St. Gallen, Aargau, and Thurgau are German-speaking. Only three are bilingual, German and French being spoken in the cantons of Bern, Fribourg, and Valais; and one is trilingual—German, Italian, and Romansch being spoken in the Grisons (see Figure 1).

The federal principle and the geographical concentration of the languages have given rise to the principle of territoriality (*Territorialitätsprinzip* or *Territorialprinzip*): The four national languages are not only guaranteed public usage, but furthermore, each language territory has the right to protect and defend its own linguistic character and to insure its survival (Schäppi, 1971:59). The principle of territoriality is not expressly guaranteed in the Constitution. However, as the Swiss jurist Walter Burckhardt has noted:

> It is now a tacitly recognized principle that each locality should be able to retain its traditional language regardless of immigrants of other languages, and consequently that linguistic boundaries once settled should not be shifted, neither to the detriment of the majority nor of minorities. It is trust in this tacit agreement that provides a foundation for peaceful relations among the language groups. Each group must be sure that the others do not wish to make conquests at its expense and diminish its territory, either officially or by private action. Adherence to this rule, as well as respect of each group for the individuality of the others, is an obligation of Swiss loyalty. It is no less sacred because it is not laid down in law; it is one of the foundations of our state itself.[3]

Swiss authors refer to the ability of the canton to regulate all cantonal affairs involving language which are not explicitly designated to the federal government as *"kantonale Sprachhoheit"* or linguistic sovereignty. Thus the canton (in accordance with the principle of territoriality) determines the official cantonal language (or in a few cases, languages). The cantonal language is the medium of instruction in the public schools. In addition, all cantonal laws and regulations are issued only in the official language(s). While compromises are made in practice, the cantons have no legal obligation to provide translations or deal with citizens in languages other than their own.

In contrast to the principle of territoriality, which operates at the cantonal level, is the principle of personality (*Personalitätsprinzip*), on the federal level, which regulates relations between the individual and the federal government. According to Article 116 of the Constitution, in direct dealings between the citizen and the Confederation, and vice versa, the federal government must adapt to the language of the individual within the limits of the official languages.

As we have previously noted, "German, French, and Italian are the official languages of the Confederation." This simple provision has been construed to allow for the complete equality of the languages. Members of both Swiss houses of parliament are

3. Walter Burckhardt, *Kommentar der schweizerischen Bundesverfassung*, quoted in McRae (1964:11-12). See also Hegnauer (1947:56) and Pedrazzini (1952:114).

TABLE 3. Percentage of Protestants and Catholics in the populations of the Swiss cantons, 1837-1970

Cantons	Protestants						Catholics					
	1837	1860	1888	1910	1941	1970	1837	1860	1888	1910	1941	1970
Appenzell Outer Rhoden	100.0%	95.4%	91.6%	88.0%	86.6%	69.8%	0.0%	4.5%	8.2%	11.8%	13.0%	27.6%
Zurich	99.6	95.3	87.1	75.9	74.5	59.5	0.4	4.2	11.8	21.8	23.1	36.7
Schaffhausen	99.0	92.8	86.9	77.8	78.2	64.2	1.0	7.0	12.6	21.8	21.0	31.9
Vaud	98.1	93.6	90.9	82.0	82.1	60.7	1.9	6.0	8.7	16.3	16.7	36.1
Neuchâtel	95.9	88.3	87.3	84.2	83.5	57.9	4.1	10.6	11.5	13.9	15.2	38.4
Basel-Land	94.2	80.7	78.6	74.8	75.3	57.7	5.8	18.9	20.9	24.7	23.8	39.1
Bern	87.0	86.8	87.0	84.9	85.8	75.2	13.0	12.5	12.5	14.2	13.6	23.3
Glarus	86.4	82.7	76.7	72.0	68.4	55.5	13.6	17.2	23.1	27.9	31.4	49.3
Basel-Stadt	85.0	75.0	67.9	63.7	64.9	52.7	15.0	24.0	30.0	33.5	30.7	40.7
Thurgau	76.2	75.2	70.9	63.4	67.0	55.0	23.8	24.4	28.9	35.9	32.6	43.5
Geneva	62.6	48.3	48.3	45.5	54.6	38.0	37.4	50.8	49.6	49.6	41.8	53.4
Grisons	61.6	56.0	54.8	51.0	51.5	45.9	38.4	44.0	45.1	48.6	48.0	52.9
Aargau	51.6	53.6	54.9	55.7	57.8	47.3	48.4	45.5	44.4	43.6	41.5	48.8
St. Gallen	37.0	38.5	40.4	38.3	39.8	34.8	63.0	61.4	59.3	60.9	59.4	63.6
Fribourg	9.9	14.7	15.6	13.7	13.4	13.4	90.1	85.3	84.3	86.1	86.3	85.8

TABLE 3 cont.

Cantons	Protestants						Catholics					
	1837	1860	1888	1910	1941	1970	1837	1860	1888	1910	1941	1970
Solothurn	9.5	13.8	25.3	33.3	40.5	37.3	90.5	86.1	74.4	66.1	58.6	59.1
Lucerne	4.4	2.0	5.7	10.2	13.0	13.4	95.6	98.0	94.1	89.1	86.2	85.2
Valais	0.4	0.8	0.8	2.3	3.6	4.4	99.6	99.2	99.2	97.0	96.1	94.9
Zug	0.0	3.1	5.9	9.1	14.8	17.4	100.0	96.8	93.9	90.7	84.9	80.6
Schwyz	0.0	1.2	2.0	4.0	6.5	7.9	100.0	98.8	98.0	95.9	93.4	91.3
Appenzell Inner Rhoden	0.0	1.0	5.2	6.3	3.8	4.7	100.0	99.0	94.8	93.7	96.0	94.9
Obwalden	0.0	0.7	2.2	3.0	4.0	4.2	100.0	99.3	97.8	97.0	95.9	95.4
Uri	0.0	0.3	2.1	5.7	8.3	6.6	100.0	99.7	97.8	94.1	91.6	93.1
Nidwalden	0.0	0.4	0.9	1.7	6.8	8.9	100.0	99.6	99.1	98.3	93.0	90.2
Ticino	0.0	0.1	0.8	2.4	5.5	7.8	100.0	99.9	98.9	94.0	92.6	89.8

Sources: Bickel (1947:299) and *Annuaire Statistique de la Suisse* (1976:36).

free to speak in the language of their choice. The texts of federal laws are published in all three languages, and all three texts have equal status before the courts. However, because Italian (which is spoken by only 4 percent of Swiss citizens) is the weakest of the three official languages, and is not understood by a majority of French- and German-speakers, it suffers practical disadvantages in both the public and governmental spheres (McRae, 1964:18-19, 24-25).

In 1938 Romansch was recognized as the fourth "national language." As opposed to the three "official languages," it does not have official status in the parliamentary, administrative, and judicial spheres of the federal government. The group that campaigned for recognition of Romansch as one of the national languages of Switzerland was aware of the burden and expense of an additional administrative language. It wanted a commitment to the principle of a fourth national language rather than to have Romansch recognized as an official language. By adopting a referendum to this effect, the Swiss people stressed the political and cultural importance of the Latin element in the Confederation, and in so doing they helped to neutralize the effects of irredentist propaganda emanating from Fascist Italy which claimed that Romansch dialects were forms of Italian. Currently the Confederation authorizes yearly sums for the preservation and furtherance of the cultural and linguistic individuality of the Ticino and the Italian- and Romansch-speaking communities of the Grisons.[4]

At the cantonal level, there has been a tendency toward equality of languages in the multilingual cantons. However, even today this equality is not in all cases complete. The Grisons have had a long history of peaceful relations among the German-speaking majority and the Romansch- and Italian-speaking minorities. Of the four multilingual cantons, it is the only one that has never been ruled by one linguistic group (Weilenmann, 1925:153). It is also noted for its extreme local autonomy, wherein the local communities are able to a considerable degree to regulate their own affairs regarding language and other matters, most notably the

4. In 1970 the annual subsidy to the Ticino and the Italian valleys of the Grisons was 285,000 Swiss francs, while the Romansch-speaking group in the Grisons received a yearly sum of 190,000 Swiss francs. The general aim of these federal grants is to protect and strengthen the cultural and linguistic heritage of the region. This includes a wide range of activities including courses on language and literature, encouragement of writers and artists, subsidies for publication, etc. Although the sums have increased slightly in recent years, especially for the Romansch-speaking group, the psychological value of federal support often seems more valuable than the monetary sum. See Schäppi (1971).

schools (Casaulta, 1966:41; Allemann, 1968:537, 548). While German, Italian, and Romansch are all official cantonal languages, and although each language group is more or less proportionately represented in official positions, in practice Romansch suffers serious disabilities in the publication of laws and decrees, in cantonal administration, and in the courts. German is the main working language of the cantonal authorities, and only the German version of cantonal laws is recognized as authentic in the courts. Nevertheless, the German-speakers in the Grisons make no effort to exert political power over the smaller language groups.

In Bern, the problems of bilingualism arose as a consequence of the annexation of the Jura district in 1815, when the victorious powers at the Congress of Vienna awarded the predominantly French-speaking Jura, the old ecclesiastical principality of Basel, to Bern in compensation for Vaud and Aargau which were taken away. The Jura was not consulted about this decision. After years of at least latent tension, the predominantly Catholic French-speaking section of the Jura was granted autonomy on January 1, 1979. Antagonism between the new canton of Jura and the remainder of the Jura districts that voted to stay with the old canton of Bern still remains. The issue of autonomy rather than linguistic grievances seems to be the thrust of the problem. French became recognized as an official language of Bern in the liberal Constitution of 1931, but full equality of the languages (including authenticity of both languages in courts of laws) did not occur until 1950.

In Valais, both French and German were declared official cantonal languages in its 1844 Constitution. Up until the French Revolution, however, the German-speaking Oberwalliser were politically dominant over the French-speakers, and there was considerable tension between the language groups. The current situation is one of language peace. Both languages are used in public life, and the two groups are proportionately represented in elective and appointive positions. The legal status of the two languages is also equal, with both texts of a law considered authentic by the courts (Grichting, 1959:74-80).

Fribourg, like Valais, was ruled by a German-speaking population until the French Revolution, and was marked by linguistic conflicts in the first part of the nineteenth century. However, in contrast to Valais, the French majority when it came to power after 1830 attempted to dominate the German Fribourgers. It made French the only official language of the canton, and the only language to be used in civil courts. With the reaction of 1814, German once again became dominant, while the liberal Constitution of 1831 turned the tables once more, making French the official language of the canton. Only in 1857 were both German and French admitted as administrative languages (Weilenmann, 1925:212-215). Even today the French text of cantonal laws is considered authoritative.

Communal autonomy helps to safeguard linguistic minorities in the multilingual cantons. Here the principle of territoriality finds application, so that in most of these communities only one language is spoken. This insures that local communities can preserve their own identity. In predominantly French-speaking Valais and Fribourg, which tend to see themselves as part of French Switzerland and are sensitive to their minority-language position in the Confederation as a whole, the minority-protecting function of local autonomy benefits the German language group, which constitutes almost one-third of the population in both cantons. Communal autonomy is also important for the Romansch-speaking groups, which comprise a majority only when the smallest unit of government is taken into consideration. On the level of the next-highest administrative unit, the district (*Kreis*), we find only three Romansch-speaking *Kreise*. However, when communes are considered, there are 76 in which Romansch-speakers comprise over 70 percent of the population (Schäppi, 1971:143-144).

Religious as well as linguistic pluralism is closely linked with federalism in Switzerland. Although the principle of territoriality no longer holds in matters of religion, it was a ruling principle until 1848.[5] The Reformation divided the Confederation into two hostile camps. After the second Kappel War in 1531, this situation was resolved in an uneasy peace that established the principle that each "sovereign" canton decided on its own religion. There were in fact, if not in law, two Confederations then—one Catholic, the other Protestant. The Catholic cantons, allied in a separate league since 1586, had a Diet of their own in Lucerne, while the Protestant cantons had theirs in Aarau.

As we have observed, it was not until 1848 that the two major faiths were reconciled. The Constitution of 1848 broke down the main barriers that had separated the Swiss cantons for over 300

5. Hughes (1975:75) comments that since 1848 the personal principle has prevailed over the territorial in religion, while with language the territorial has taken precedence over the personal. Previously, the positions were reversed: "The old regime dealt with the religious problem on the territorial principle, and the language problem on the personal principle—the Bernese spoke French to their Vaudois subjects, and the administration of the Italian bailiwicks was chiefly in Italian." The Catholic religion, however, was unlawful in the Protestant territories, as was the reformed in the Catholic ones.

years. It guaranteed the right of migration to Swiss of both Christian faiths. The Jews, however, did not gain full equality of citizenship until 1866. Until 1973, the Constitution also contained articles banning the Jesuits and prohibiting the establishment of new monasteries or religious orders. These provisions were specifically directed against the Catholic Church and were influenced by the *Kulturkampf* (a struggle between the Catholic Church and the lay powers of the state) and the excitement created in Switzerland by the Pope's proclamation of infallibility. Today the majority of cantons provides for the legal recognition of the two major churches. Religious intolerance has given way to tolerance and freedom of worship for all faiths, as guaranteed in the Constitution.

Under the Federal Constitution, matters pertaining to primary education and marriage,[6] and the registration of births and deaths, are under the jurisdiction of the federal government. However, in keeping with the decentralized and federal character of the Swiss state, the cantons are free to pass laws concerning state-church relations so long as they do not violate the freedoms and rights mentioned in the Federal Constitution. They may create a single state church, or many, or none, as they deem appropriate. Although control of the public schools must come under the civil authority, this does not exclude priests from participating as members of school boards or on cantonal supervisory commissions (Stöckli, 1970:42). Freedom of religion is not so much a principle for shaping the public schools and their educational system, but rather, negatively, a guarantee for the individual, that his religious freedom shall be preserved in the school. Article 27 states that:

> The public schools shall be such that they may be attended by adherents of any religious confession without any offense to their freedom of belief and conscience.

Instruction—with the exception of religious classes, which are not compulsory—must in matters of faith be neutral. But this protection is relative. It does not mean that the instruction has to be unreligious. It is quite possible for clergymen (with the previous long-standing exception of the Jesuits) to be teachers. This is, in fact, very much the case in the rural areas of the Catholic

6. Codding (1961:52) notes that the right to marry "was placed under the protection of the Confederation to curb earlier practices of the Catholic church. As a result, the civil ceremony of marriage is the only one legal in the eyes of the law." Burial laws were likewise deconfessionalized.

cantons. Article 27 does not require that each public school has to be open to students of all faiths—although this is by far the predominant practice—but only that, for each faith, a public school has to be open which does not offend the above-stated principle. This compromise allows the Catholic cantons to preserve their identity without either offending the principle of the separation of church and state, which has often been a source of contention between the liberal urban Protestant cantons and the more conservative rural Catholic cantons, or having to resort to two school systems, as is the case in Canada.

Organization of the army is also influenced by the federal principle and traditions of the old Confederation. Article 21 of the Constitution requires that army units must be formed from men of the same canton "unless military considerations stand in the way." By having the canton as a basis of organization, there is a tendency for units as well as regiments and even divisions to be linguistically homogeneous. On the other hand, bilingual and in a few cases trilingual units are necessary at a considerably lower level in certain linguistically mixed cantons and in specialized services.

Army service, which is universal and compulsory, has a strong nationalizing influence. The recruit school brings the young men of the country together at a very impressionable age. Besides informal civic instruction which stresses the Swiss national position and attitude, it introduces Swiss, from whatever linguistic group, to the varied landscape of their country, and gives them something in common to talk about for the rest of their lives.

The army's general principle of language usage is that each soldier and noncommissioned officer should be instructed in his own language. This practice, however, breaks down for the small Romansch-speaking group, which is instructed in either German or Italian. In contrast, officers are expected to have an adequate knowledge of two or three languages as a condition of their commission. All important army manuals and regulations, like federal laws and decrees, are published in the three official languages.

Through the federal system of government, the linguistic and religious minorities have been able to protect substantially autonomous bases for their own cultures. The system of local autonomy, coupled with a high ethnic concentration, allows most Swiss to live in relatively homogeneous territories, even though they are citizens of a highly diversified nation. Hans Huber (1946:10), a past Justice of the Swiss Federal Supreme Court, has noted that the purpose of the federal structure is to protect linguistic and cultural minorities. However, most institutions are not aimed primarily at giving protection to minorities against majorities. Rather, they are pillars of the Swiss federal system, and their minority-protecting functions are a fortuitous by-product.

In addition, federalism as practiced in Switzerland today has multiple effects on the moderation of political conflict. By granting substantial powers to the cantons, the Constitution not only provides for an elaborate set of checks and balances, but also "gives its seal to a horizontal segmentation of social and political life" (Kerr, 1974:27-31 and 1975:7; Lijphart, 1977a). Many issues are mediated on the cantonal or communal level which might be more intractable at the national level.

Nevertheless, while the laws and institutional arrangements governing linguistic and religious minorities in the Confederation do provide the necessary preconditions for the well-being of minorities, they do not completely explain the secret of Swiss coexistence. To grasp with any clarity the interrelationship between the linguistic and religious groups, one must turn to the social milieu within which they interact.

Informal Practices and Social Patterns

One of the most notable factors in the realm of language is the widespread use of dialect in German-speaking Switzerland. This, oddly enough, has many important consequences for the relations between the majority and minority language groups. There are over 20 different German Swiss dialects that can be distinguished. They differ both from each other and from high German (Schwarzenbach, 1969). Swiss German or *Schwyzerdütsch*, in one of its many forms, is the normal language of the German Swiss in daily life and at all levels of society. Although Swiss German does not enjoy official recognition, the German-speaking cantons hold tenaciously to their own dialects as a means of preserving their individual identity. One of the consequences of this diversity within German Switzerland is that it is viewed as less threatening in the eyes of the other language groups than a monolithic language block of the same size would be.

While all German Swiss children learn high German in school, it is simply never used in ordinary conversation. When ninth-grade students and their teachers were asked their opinion about dialect and high German, they replied that the dialect was more sympathetic, honest, and personal, as well as easier to understand and express oneself in. In addition, it gave them the feeling of belonging together. In contrast, high German was constraining, artificial, and formal (Joos, 1974). The tension between "speaking a language they do not write, and writing a language they seldom speak" may well give German Swiss more motivation to learn additional languages.

The Italian- and Romansch-speaking Swiss also have their own dialects. The Ticinesi learn standard Italian in the schools, just as the German Swiss learn high German. On the other hand, Romansch is sufficiently distinct in the different mountain valleys that cantonal authorities publish elementary school texts in four different Romansch idioms. The two main forms of Romansch are Surselvisch, spoken in the predominantly Catholic gorges of the Rhine, and Ladin, spoken in the Engadin. Between the two areas are Sutselvisch and Surmeirisch, which only became written languages in modern times (Peer and Pult, 1974; Peer, 1975).

Unlike the other Swiss groups, the French Swiss do not, on the whole, speak a dialect. Their language, like that of the French-speaking Belgian Walloons, is simply a regional variation of standard French. Siegfried (1956:63) remarked in 1950 that while "there are Franco-Provencal patois in use between the Jura and the Alps, for the French-speaking Swiss the French tongue is something quite different from what German is for the Alemanic Swiss. French is both a spoken and a written language for the Swiss Romands. It is not merely a language for familiar everyday use, but one for cultural and business affairs as well."

Although in everyday dealings the average Swiss citizen is usually in the presence of others who share his mother tongue, when Swiss of different language groups converse, either face to face or through written correspondence, pluralingualism is put to a test. There has been little research on bi- and multilingualism in Switzerland; however, one cannot fail to notice that many Swiss have a command of one or more foreign languages. In a recent representative sample of French- and German-speaking Swiss aged 20 or older, two-thirds had a working knowledge of at least one other official language: 65 percent of the German Swiss had a knowledge of French, while 52 percent of the French Swiss had a command of German (Scope Institute, 1973:8, 11). This fact has important consequences for the linguistic situation in Switzerland.

For many reasons—numerical, psychological, and social/political—the most important majority-minority relation in Switzerland today is that between French- and German-speaking Swiss. Therefore, it is significant that when French and German Swiss speak together, or correspond with one another, the language is most apt to be French, not merely in French Switzerland but in German Switzerland as well. In part, this is done as a courtesy to a minority language group. However, this explanation is not adequate, for this courtesy is not extended to the other minority languages. Two factors appear to explain this tendency. First, as we have seen, there is the obvious factor of competence—more German Swiss have some knowledge of French than do French Swiss of German. Second is the prestige of the French language in Switzerland, which, as McRae (1964:17) observes, "serves as an effective counterbalance to its numerical weakness." This prestige can be traced back to the use of French by ruling aristocracies in several German cantons from the seventeenth to the end of the eighteenth century, and to its use long afterward as the language of culture and diplomacy. The relative decline in the international prestige of French has not been felt as severely in Switzerland as in some other countries. One prime reason for this situation is the horror with which the Swiss viewed the period of Nazi domination in Germany; this destroyed all traces of pan-Germanism in cultural and linguistic matters, and thus most of the incentive to assert the merits of the German language and civilization vis-à-vis the French culture.

Although French is now facing strong competition from English, German Swiss endeavor to learn French, sometimes spending a *"Welschlandjahr"* in French Switzerland for this purpose. The French Swiss seldom reciprocate on this point,[7] both because they find the Swiss German dialects difficult to grasp and because they prefer to learn *"le bon allemand."* Even when a French Swiss is capable of speaking German, he will usually attempt to converse in French. A French-speaking teacher from Biel told me he always started conversations in public places in French, resorting to German only if necessary, despite the fact that he spoke both fluent high German and dialect. Nevertheless, he was concerned about the French and German language groups going their separate ways in Biel, and was looking into the possibility of having German and French secondary students combine for art and physical education classes. This illustrates some of the paradoxes of the Swiss language situation.

7. *"Welsche"* (originally meaning "foreign") is the word used by the German Swiss to describe the French Swiss. A recent exchange program between young adults in French and German Switzerland met with a qualified success: few Romands applied for the project, while there were many willing German Swiss. See *Der Brückenbauer*, Jan. 1, 1977 (Zurich).

Another informal language practice which deserves mention is the use of high German, rather than dialect, on occasions when German Swiss address their fellow citizens of other languages in their own tongue. This is done as a convenience and a courtesy to the other language groups, who would have more difficulty understanding dialect.[8] On less formal occasions, such as when a compatriot of another language group or a foreigner asks directions, the German Swiss also almost always replies in high German.

Informally, as well as in administrative and judicial matters, the linguistic territories are recognized. For example, the ticket collector walks down the train calling for tickets in German until the invisible frontier is passed, at which time he continues through the train in French. Furthermore, infringements of other languages in their territorial space—particularly in the minority language areas of French and Italian—are likely to come under fire. There was a loud protest when the restaurant chain *"Silberkugel"* wanted to open a branch under its German name in Lausanne (*National Zeitung*, Basel, Oct. 16, 1976).[9] In the Ticino, threatened by an onslaught of *germanizzazione*, a particularly dramatic measure was taken. The canton in 1931 passed a language decree insisting that Italian signs precede any other language, and that any translations be limited to letters no more than half the size of the Italian. In addition, these signs were subject to a small tax.[10]

Italian—in contrast to French and German, which meet on more or less equal terms—is spoken by relatively few French- and German-speaking Swiss. Thus the Italian Swiss must be fluent in either French or German, or both, for any career that transcends the purely local level. For professional jobs this condition becomes a necessity, since there are no Italian-language universities in Switzerland,[11] although there are two chairs in Ticino law at the

8. One exception to this situation occurs in the canton of Bern. The Bernese have had a long tradition of speaking *Bärndütsch* in the Grand Council. While this practice reinforces the peculiar identity of Bern, at the same time it has irritated the French-speaking Jurassians. See Hadorn et al. (1971:18).

9. There appears to be more sensitivity about German than about other languages. A McDonald's hamburger stand was constructed in Geneva without comment. Whether this is due to the more international atmosphere of Geneva or to the lesser sensitivity to the English language is difficult to ascertain.

10. The Federal Tribunal later ruled that while cantons are legally competent to regulate language usage, it would be against the spirit of the Federal Constitution without compelling reasons. Only the restriction on the letter size of words was struck down.

11. There is, of course, the possibility of attending university in Italy. The question of an Italian-language university has been discussed for over a century.

University of Bern and some classes (particularly introductory courses in science and technology and those of a cultural nature) are offered at the Federal Institute of Technology in Zurich. In fact, many Ticinesi are fluent in German and French, and assimilate rapidly in a German or French milieu. The opposite, however, is less true; particularly when the German Swiss migrates to the Ticino, assimilation proceeds much more slowly.

The position of Romansch is even more precarious than Italian. Although a few classes are offered at the *Volkshochschule* in Zurich, a negligible number of other Swiss learn the language. Thus, the Romansch Swiss must adjust to the use of a second language everywhere he turns outside of a few mountain valleys in the Grisons. In general, Romansch speakers have met this challenge, and are known for their mastery of other languages. It follows that they easily adapt to a new language milieu. On the other hand, when the German Swiss moves to the Grisons, it is the Romansch Swiss who faces the greater risk of assimilation by the far stronger German culture. In some cases, communal autonomy has proved a danger rather than a safeguard to the survival of Romansch. For it is the privilege of a community to change its school language, which quite a few have done in recent years, preferring the utility of German to the limited usage of Romansch. This problem is exacerbated by the fact that there are limited possibilities for jobs in the Romansch-speaking areas. The extent of this problem becomes obvious when one realizes that over 2,500 Romansch-speaking people live in Zurich, where they are more numerous than in any other commune with the exception of Chur (3,000), and that approximately one-fourth of the 50,000 Romansch-speakers live in German or French Switzerland or abroad (Hughes, 1975:58; Peer and Pult, 1974:4). Table 4 illustrates the difficulty of preserving the Romansch tongue, even on its home ground.

From an economic standpoint, there are no outstanding disparities between French and German Switzerland (see Table 5). Three of the monolingual French-speaking cantons (Geneva, Vaud, and Neuchâtel) have per capita incomes which are above the majority of German-speaking cantons (statistics are not available for Jura). On the other hand, the two predominantly French-speaking cantons of Valais and Fribourg are considerably below most of the German-speaking cantons, and even below Italian-

---

The general consensus seems to be that the Ticino does not have the financial means to support one. See Pedrazzini (1952).

TABLE 4. Romansch-speakers in the
Confederation and the canton of Grisons

	Swiss population	Romansch	Percentage
1941	4,265,703	46,456	1.1%
1950	4,714,992	48,862	1.0
1960	5,429,061	49,823	0.9
1970	6,269,783	50,339	0.8
	Population of Grisons	Romansch	Percentage
1941	128,247	40,187	31.3%
1950	137,100	40,109	29.2
1960	147,458	38,414	26.1
1970	162,086	37,878	23.4

Source: Steinberg (1976:115).

speaking Ticino. It is noteworthy that the disparities are far greater within each linguistic group than between them. On the whole,
French Switzerland is economically represented in almost exact
proportion to its numerical strength. In 1975 the French Swiss
comprised approximately 20 percent of the Swiss population, produced 22.4 percent of the Swiss national product, and earned 22.7
percent of the income received in Switzerland, an average of
19,297 Swiss francs per capita compared to 19,036 Swiss francs
per capita for Switzerland as a whole (*Tages Anzeiger*, Zurich, foreign edition, Dec. 21, 1976). Even the major cities are well distributed, with two of the five largest in French Switzerland (Geneva
and Lausanne) and three in German Switzerland (Zurich, Basel,
and Bern).

On the other hand, some French Swiss feel that much of the
real economic wealth and power is located east of the Sarne in
Zurich, Basel, and Bern, and that many key posts in Swiss industry are monopolized by German-speakers. However, when a national sample of Swiss was asked whether they believed the
political influence of employers was too large, about right, or too
small, Glass (1975:149) reports that although "French speakers
may indeed be aware of possible Germanization through com-
merce and industry, there is no evidence to indicate French-
speakers believe such Germanization actually characterizes the
present-day situation."

TABLE 5. *Average cantonal income and gross products, 1975*

Canton	Average per capita income in Swiss francs	Relation-ship to the Swiss average	Gross cantonal product in millions of Swiss francs	Per-centage of Swiss national product
Basel-Stadt	32,831	172%	7,163.7	5.87%
Geneva	27,128	143	9,190.8	7.54
Zug	26,886	141	1,978.8	1.62
Zurich	23,245	122	26,269.9	21.57
Basel-Land	20,113	106	4,471.1	3.67
Vaud	18,771	99	9.883.1	8.11
Glarus	18,614	98	685.0	0.56
Schaffhausen	18,273	96	1,306.5	1.07
Aargau	18,262	96	8,190.3	6.72
Neuchâtel	18,169	95	3,054.2	2.51
Solothurn	17,627	93	4,011.9	3.29
Bern	16,585	87	16,568.9	13.59
Nidwalden	16,023	84	429.4	0.35
Thurgau	15,964	84	2,982.2	2.45
Ticino	15,910	84	4,240.1	3.48
Grisons	15,901	84	2,649.1	2.17
Lucerne	15,468	81	4,550.6	3.73
Appenzell Outer Rhoden	15,330	81	735.8	0.60
St. Gallen	15,199	80	5,904.8	4.84
Valais	14,494	76	3,126.4	2.56
Schwyz	13,102	69	1,223.8	1.00
Uri	13,132	69	453.1	0.37
Fribourg	12,996	68	2,371.7	1.95
Obwalden	11,739	62	302.9	0.25
Appenzell Inner Rhoden	11,398	60	153.9	0.13

Source: Schweizerische Bankgesellschaft (1976).

In contrast to French and German Switzerland, Italian Switzerland is poor, although among all the cantons it ranks in approximately the lower middle range. It has no major industries and only limited agricultural land. In recent years Ticino has attracted many tourists and new residents from German Switzerland and Germany; but although this has brought needed revenues, it has also intensified the weak linguistic position Italian Switzerland occupies in the Confederation. Despite this, the relationship between German Switzerland and Ticino does not have only negative aspects. A strong feeling of togetherness also plays a role, a feeling which Vollenweider (1975:74) characterizes as "stronger between the Ticino and German Switzerland than between German and French Switzerland."

From a cultural standpoint, it is of considerable significance that Switzerland's three official languages are of major and approximately equal importance. German, French, and Italian Swiss accept the culture of Germany, France, or Italy as their own and contribute to the literary life of their respective language group. Nevertheless, as Brooks (1930:186-187) notes, Swiss instructors emphasize the part played by their own countrymen and reject the chauvinistic excesses accompanying the foreign culture abroad, distinguishing sharply between the culture and the political organization of other nations.

An old and often-asked question is whether there exists a Swiss culture (see Fick, 1919). The Swiss literary traditions differ very little from those of the three larger cultures with which they interact. On the other hand, Swiss of all language groups seem to share certain values that are foreign to their cultural kin outside Switzerland. These include a devotion to local autonomy and particularisms, as well as to direct democracy. We shall consider the values and attitudes that both unite and separate the two largest linguistic groups in a later chapter.

Unlike the informal linguistic patterns in Switzerland, the religious patterns are more difficult to characterize. Returning once again to Table 5, we observe that per capita income in the predominantly Catholic cantons, with the exception of Zug, is lower than in the majority of old Protestant cantons. The Catholic cantons are, on the whole, rural and mountainous, and lack an industrial base. Although in 1970 nine and one-half cantons (including Appenzell Inner Rhoden) remained overwhelmingly Catholic (90 percent or more), they encompassed only 34 percent of all Catholics in Switzerland. While no statistics are available, it appears that Catholics who have migrated to the industrial cantons share the same high standard of living as their Protestant neighbors. One survey also indicates that religious differences do not seem to have any effect on the values, attitudes, and ethical principles concerning basic areas of life. In 1964 Boltanski (1967) found that both Catholics and Protestants see religion as a guide to behavior and favor rigorous, authoritative education for their children, hard work and fulfillment of duty, and attitudes generally encompassed by what has come to be called the Protestant ethic.

The total rapprochement between Catholic and Protestant is a relatively new phenomenon. Andermatt (1972) has traced the slow evolution of Swiss Catholics out of the ghetto and toward full integration into Swiss society. After considerable setbacks, a critical period came in the first two decades of the twentieth century with the founding of the *Schweizerischen Katholischen Volksverein* in 1905 and the Catholic Conservative Party in 1912. This period was followed by the building of a vast associational federation that came to include hospitals, denominational schools, a Catholic trade union, and various social clubs and sports organizations. Thus Andermatt (1972:21) writes that:

> A Catholic might be born in a Catholic hospital, attend Catholic schools from kindergarten to university, read Catholic newspapers and magazines, and vote for the Catholic party and take part in Catholic clubs or associations. It was not unusual for a Catholic to insure himself against sickness or accident with a Catholic company and put his savings in a Catholic savings bank.

Gradually, the organizational completeness and recognition of the strength of these institutions enabled members of the Catholic subculture to participate with growing confidence in the hitherto liberal-dominated and secular federal political arena, and finally to gain acceptance and complete integration into the larger society. This pattern of withdrawal into a ghetto, which provides self-confidence and economic support as a means to integration into the larger society, is a familiar one in the annals of ethnic relations in the United States.[12]

12. See, for example, Glazer and Moynihan, *Beyond the Melting Pot* (1970). Black nationalism may also be seen as a step up the ethnic ladder to full participation in American society. Hamilton and Carmichael (1967:44) seem to advance this interpretation when they observe:

The concept of Black power rests on a fundamental premise: Before a group can enter the open society, it must first close ranks. By this we mean that group solidarity is necessary before a group can operate effectively from a bargaining position of strength in a pluralistic society. Traditionally, each new ethnic group in society has found the route to social and political viability

The linguistic cleavage has never reached the intensity of the religious one. Still, a strong pull of conflicting nationalisms was felt during the early years of the twentieth century. Swiss Germans venerated the new Germany produced by Bismarck and looked admiringly toward Heidelberg and Berlin. These attitudes were not shared or comprehended in French Switzerland. A strong wave of irredentism in Italy, which was directed in turn against parts of Austria and southern Switzerland, found support among a small radical circle of intellectuals in the Ticino. The outbreak of World War I in 1914 found Switzerland divided between its three linguistic and cultural groups. A deep fissure which came to be known as the trench, or *Graben*, opened between French and German Switzerland and threatened to destroy the moral unity of the country. The Swiss Federal Council found it necessary in an appeal on October 1, 1914, to reassert "the ideal of our country as a cultural community and as a political idea above the diversity of race and language" (Kohn, 1956:128). Carl Spitteler, a famous Swiss poet, re-echoed this sentiment in 1914 in an address before the New Helvetic Society entitled *"Unser Schweizer Standpunkt."* As the war dragged on, relations between French and German Switzerland became entangled with the issue of neutrality. General Ulrich Wille came under suspicion for his pro-German bias, and Arthur Hoffman, the Federal Councillor who headed the Political (foreign) Office, was finally forced to resign for his breach of neutrality. However, by deliberate effort and self-control, neutrality was preserved and the country was precariously held together.

Twenty years later, when World War II approached, Switzerland found herself in a strategically more precarious but intellectually more secure position than in 1914. The rise of the European dictatorships led to a reinforcement of national unity. Italian and German Switzerland recoiled against the savage nationalism propagated in Italy and Germany. Even the ties between French Switzerland and France cooled down after the establishment of the Vichy regime. McRae (1964:22) observes that "wartime isolation was temporary, but the unity that it fostered has been more lasting. If Switzerland's three main cultures have had in recent years a community of outlook that they have never known previously, they owe it in no small measure to the threat levelled against them by Hitler and Mussolini."[13] The decades after World

---

through the organization of its own institutions with which to represent its needs within the larger society.

13. External threats have, on many occasions, united the Swiss cultural and religious groups. In fact, this is a recurrent theme in Swiss history.

War II have brought some critics to question whether this commonality of outlook still prevails. Some social observers maintain that there is currently a general "Helvetic malaise" in Switzerland.[14]

Recognition of Minorities

Part of the secret of Swiss cultural coexistence is recognition and often overrepresentation of the minority linguistic and religious groups. The Federal Council, which is elected by parliament to a four-year term, is composed of seven members from the four major parties: two Liberals, two from the Christian Popular Party, two Socialists, and one from the Swiss Popular Party. This allocation of positions on the Federal Council (which has been called the Magic Formula) is roughly proportional to the parties' share of the popular vote. The practice of having all or most major parties represented on the Council has a long tradition in Swiss political history. The last step was taken in 1959 when the Socialists were accorded a proportionate share of seats.

Efforts are also made to include individuals who represent not only the largest parties but also the various subcultures in Swiss society. The constitution provides that no two Federal Councillors may come from the same canton. But a complex network of rules has, in fact, shaped the pattern of representation. Zurich, Bern, and Vaud have been almost continuously represented since 1848, with the Vaud seat assuring at least one French-speaking Councillor. Generally there are two non-Germans, with a seat occasionally going to a Ticinese.[15] Two Catholic seats are assured by the composition of the parties, the Christian Popular Party members naturally choosing Catholics. The Liberals and the Swiss Popular Party members select Protestants, and the Socialists choose a personality whose confessional loyalty is not too pronounced (Hughes, 1962:74-80). Thus the collegial executive may be considered as an expression of the linguistic, religious, and regional differences within Swiss society.

Similar conventions for representation of the diversity of language and religion also apply to parliamentary committees, the judiciary, the public service, and federally supported corpora-

14. The phrase "Helvetic malaise" was coined by Imboden (1964) to describe the general discontent and preoccupation with problems of the day. See also Rohr (1972:21-22).

15. Hughes (1962:76) notes that after a turn of not being represented, an Italian-speaker (which usually means a Ticinese) obtains a strong claim to one seat.

tions.[16] For example, even the small Italian-speaking group, which comprises only 4 percent of all Swiss citizens, is overrepresented in the civil service, with 7.6 percent of all federal administrative employees, 6.0 percent of postal employees, and 11.9 percent of railway employees. Only at the upper levels of the administrative grade of the civil service is the proportion of Ticinesi and Italian Swiss from the Grisons precisely equivalent to their numbers in the population (Zenger, 1973).

Under the Swiss system of direct democracy, the electorate has the last word in most important decisions. The popular referendum provides a substantial check on the federal parliament. At the demand of 50,000 citizens, federal legislation must be submitted to the electorate for acceptance or rejection. In addition, the compulsory constitutional referendum requires that all constitutional amendments must obtain a majority of both the citizens and the cantons to succeed. The people also have a right of "initiative," which entitles any citizen or group of citizens who can obtain 100,000 signatures to propose constitutional amendments which must be considered by parliament and be submitted to a referendum. Through the referendum process, the cantons of French, Italian, and Catholic Switzerland can combine to form a majority, thus enabling them to constitute a check on the powers of the majority.

While the political map of electoral combinations in Switzerland is ever-changing, there is a recurrent tendency for French Switzerland to join forces with the Catholic cantons of German Switzerland in opposing measures they feel to be either too centralizing or threatening to cantonal autonomy (see Siegfried, 1956:193-198; Ruffieux, 1962:262-264). Thus, although the referendum process is not a device for minority recognition as such, its operation has often enabled the religious and linguistic minorities to combine for structural reasons as a defensive measure against the Protestant German, economically strong "center."

In addition to political factors, social ones also play an important role in Swiss intergroup relations. To understand how attitudes toward multiculturalism are formed, one must examine the role of the important socializing agents in Swiss society. The next chapter will concentrate on the role of the school and its curriculum.

16. Radio and television revenues, which are derived primarily from annual license fees, are distributed in larger proportion to the minority language groups than would be expected from the amount collected in French and Italian Switzerland. The radio allocations were, in 1977, 45:33:22 for the German, French, and Italian Swiss corporations, respectively.

3 | The Transmission of Values:
Ethnicity and Political Socialization in Switzerland

The school, in literate societies, is probably the most natural starting place for the investigation of how attitudes toward multiculturalism are formed. From the time of Plato, those political philosophers who stress the importance of habits, manners, and tastes as the foundation of a society have seen the paramount place of education in the politico-social order. In 1772 Rousseau, for example, wrote in *Considerations on the Government of Poland:* "It is education that must give souls a national formation, and direct their opinions and tastes in such a way that they will be patriotic by inclination, by passion, by necessity" (1953 ed.:176). He believed that only through education could there develop a spirit of nationality, patriotism, and civic responsibility. Around the turn of the twentieth century Durkheim also emphasized this theme, asserting that public schools must shape the national morality, instill the collective consciousness, and maintain national solidarity (1961 ed.:8).

Pestalozzi, on the other hand, while agreeing with Plato and Rousseau on the close relationship between education and politics, stressed the individual instead of the interests of the community as the true foundation of education and of political life. He was convinced that there is in the individual a potential faculty for liberty which should enable him to resist the temptations of his national being and of society. True civic education, according to Pestalozzi, should then aim to develop that faculty of individual liberty. Since he saw in a nation only an aggregate of individuals, and the character of this aggregate was determined by the character of the individuals which composed it, he believed that a state which promoted the autonomy of its citizens assured the strongest and most enduring basis for its own existence (see Kohn, 1956: 61-65).

The heritage of Rousseau and Pestalozzi, two countrymen of international renown, has, it would seem, made the Swiss more conscious of their educational system than many other peoples are. Several foreign observers have commented on the seriousness with which the Swiss view education (Soloveytchik, 1954; Rickover, 1962; Brooks, 1930). Brooks (1930:172) remarks that "seldom does the discussion of any political evil which arises among them proceed to any length without frequent and insistent assertions that it is due to faults in the school system of the country and it is to be cured radically only by the improvement of the latter."[1]

In order for us to understand the part played by the school in socializing interethnic sentiments, this chapter will present an overview of the Swiss educational system and its curriculum. The first section documents the complex interaction between the Swiss cultural groups and the federal system in the educational sphere. The discussion then moves to foreign-language instruction in Switzerland. Next we shall discuss the role of the school curriculum from a general comparative perspective. The second part of the chapter consists of a content analysis of Swiss secondary-school history textbooks.

An Overview of the Swiss Educational System

The historical development and political, religious, linguistic, and geographical structure of Switzerland have imposed upon it a very decentralized system of education. According to Article 27 of the Constitution, the cantons are charged with the duty of maintaining the schools. The Constitution of 1874 also made education compulsory, general, and free—every child must attend school for at least eight years, with nine years becoming common in most cantons. Within this framework, all questions relating to curricula, the methods of teaching, and the selection and appointments of teachers are in the hands of the communes and cantons. Although there are over 26 slightly different school systems, they follow a similar sequence in preparing their students for the adult world. Figure 3 is a simplified diagram of the organization of education in Switzerland.

The Swiss student first enters primary school. Thereafter, most pupils go on to secondary school—after the third year in one

1. Engeli (1972:16) links the need to study political socialization in the schools in Switzerland with the decreasing number of citizens who go to the polls.

FIGURE 3. Simplified diagram of the organization of education in Switzerland

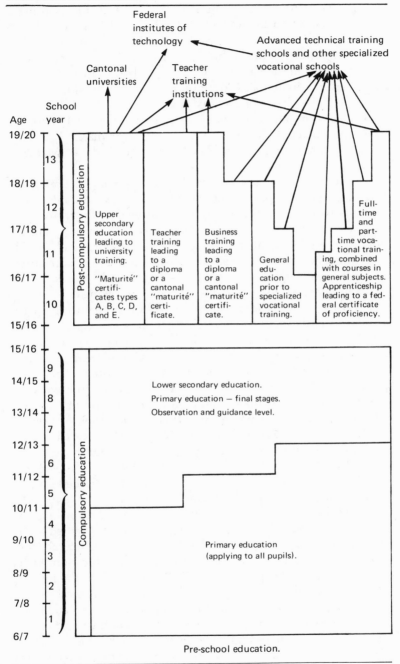

Source: Egger and Blanc (1974:14).

canton, the fourth in two, the fifth in five, and the sixth in 17 cantons (Egger and Blanc, 1974:13). The second phase of Swiss education includes the upper levels of compulsory education. The majority of students finish their formal education after nine years of schooling, and then approximately 60 percent of the males and 35 percent of the females continue to an apprenticeship program which prepares them for a skilled trade or a wide range of white-collar jobs. A minority of students (approximately 10-15 percent) enter the Mittelschulen. These include the gymnasia, lycées, or colleges which prepare students for the Federal Maturity Certificates.

As we have noted previously, the language of instruction follows in general the principle of territoriality. The assimilation of migrants from other linguistic groups, as well as children of foreign parentage, is primarily accomplished through the schools. Only in a few bilingual areas such as Biel, Fribourg, and Sion do two state school systems exist side by side to accommodate different language groups. One exception is the privately-owned French school in Bern. Although Bern is a German-speaking city situated in a wholly German-speaking region of a bilingual canton, it is also the federal capital and therefore occupies a special position as the seat of government of plurilingual Switzerland. For a long time French-speaking civil servants, who viewed their sojourn in Bern as but one phase of a career that was rooted primarily in western Switzerland, felt aggrieved that their children were denied an education in their mother tongue. On the other hand, local opinion firmly opposed any official recognition of French-language facilities as a violation of the principle of territoriality. Finally this issue was resolved by a practical compromise. A private French school which had been in existence since 1944 was incorporated as a private foundation in 1959 and awarded support by the canton and the Confederation (see McRae, 1964:67-70).

Despite the fact that education is basically a cantonal matter, it is subject to federal intervention on a few points specified by the Constitution. Article 27 establishes the principle of federal subsidies to the cantons for the support of primary education. Every canton receives a basic annual grant in proportion to the number of students aged 7 to 15, according to the latest federal census. Furthermore, the nine mountain cantons receive an additional payment per child to help cover their higher education costs and to supplement their more limited resources. Finally, the Ticino and the Grisons (which are also among the mountain cantons) receive a special linguistic supplement to help defray the heavy costs of issuing textbooks and training teachers. The total subsidy paid amounts to almost seven times the standard rate for each Italian Swiss child and over ten times for each Romansch child.

In recent years, several efforts have been made toward inter-cantonal cooperation. In the 1960s the Swiss Conference of Directors of Education attempted to harmonize the major discrepancies in the Swiss educational system by drawing a Concordat (agreement between the cantons) on School Coordination. The Concordat, which was approved unanimously by this group on October 29, 1970, came into force on June 9, 1971, following the approval of the Federal Council and the electorate in ten cantons. In particular, it proposed to set the date for entrance into school at 6 years of age, the duration of obligatory schooling to at least 9 years, with a minimum of 39 weeks of school per year, and to fix the time between entering school and the maturity examination at 12 or 13 years. It also established autumn as the beginning of the school year for all of Switzerland.[2] The agreement pledged the parties to work toward more freedom of movement for students between similar schools, common recognition of degrees and diplomas, uniformity of degrees and types of schools, a standard time for passage to the second phase of compulsory schooling, common teaching aids, and an attempt to achieve some equivalency in teacher training.

After a good start, the Concordat ran into difficulties. By 1973 twenty out of twenty-five cantons had ratified it, but among the five missing were Bern and Zurich, two of the largest cantons. According to Jean-Daniel Perret of the Neuchâtel Department of Education, the problem was not simply that two of the largest cantons did not carry out the agreement. The French-speaking cantons would continue their efforts at coordination, but the actions of Bern and Zurich could "create a new rupture between the French-speaking and the German-speaking cantons" (Fondation pour la Collaboration Confédérale, 1973:201).

In contrast with German Switzerland, the school systems in French Switzerland tend to be more harmonized. Since 1962 a number of teachers and school officials have been pressing for an

2. Currently, the starting date for schools fluctuates between cantons and even between communities in the same canton. Most schools in the French-speaking part of Switzerland begin in autumn, while those in German Switzerland tend toward spring opening dates. This presents many difficulties for students transferring from one school to another. In bilingual Biel, a practical compromise was agreed to, so that French-speaking students now begin school in the fall to coincide with the opening time in French Switzerland, while German-speaking students begin in spring.

"*Ecole Romande*" with a common curriculum. Besides facilitating coordination between schools in French Switzerland, an *Ecole Romande* is also intended to strengthen the position of the French language and culture *vis-à-vis* German Switzerland.

Foreign Language Instruction in Switzerland

Swiss scholars have called attention to the historical role of the school in promoting linguistic peace. According to Weilenmann (1962:235), the relatively high state of culture and professional education of the population, as well as the insistence on compulsory education by all the cantons since 1830, has aided this development. Of obvious importance is also the high regard accorded the learning of the other national languages. This disposition facilitates assimilation and mutual understanding and reduces prejudice.[3]

Although there are over 26 different educational systems, the introduction of the Federal Maturity Certificate has brought about a great deal of standardization of secondary, and to a certain extent primary, education. Originally established as a uniform entrance standard for courses in medicine, dentistry, pharmacy, and certain related fields, it has long been a recognized qualification for entry to a Federal Institute of Technology or to any of the faculties of the Swiss universities without further examination.[4]

The maturity certificate is gained through five different

---

3. In a recent report on the introduction and coordination of foreign-language instruction during compulsory education, one of the arguments for beginning instruction earlier in the school curriculum is that: "In plurilingual Switzerland it is necessary, for cultural-political reasons, that all children learn the language of another ethnic group. This would not only be helpful—particularly in bilingual and multilingual cantons—for purposes of communication, but could also contribute to the better understanding of fellow citizens and fellow human beings who speak other languages. An early acquisition of a foreign language can help lessen prejudices against those who speak and think differently from oneself, and perhaps even avoid their formation" (Schweizerische Konferenz der kantonalen Erziehungsdirektoren, 1976:6).

4. Although secondary education is not the concern of the Confederation, it was nevertheless obliged to legislate in this connection on account of Article 33, which provided that the cantons may require "proof of competence" from anyone who intends to engage in a liberal profession. Under the authority of these articles, the Swiss government passed a law in 1877 on the freedom of domicile of medical personnel, which permitted the Federal Council to issue a series of decrees which established the maturity certificate as a prerequisite for enrollment in schools of medicine, dentistry, pharmacy, and veterinary medicine.

courses of study. In addition to certain core subjects,[5] the classical stream (Type A) requires two official languages plus Latin and Greek. The modern language streams, as well as the scientific and commercial streams, require two official languages plus a third official language or English. Furthermore, for Type B, Latin is required; for Type C, descriptive geometry; for Type D, a fourth language (in addition to the above three), which may include English, a third official language, or another modern language (Spanish or Russian); and for Type E, economic sciences.

The general pattern is that French is studied in German and Italian Switzerland, while German is studied in French Switzerland. For those who are in the modern language or scientific stream, Italian has fought a losing battle with English in most cantons. The only group that regularly learns all three official languages is Italian-speaking Swiss gymnasium students. This situation was in some small way remedied by the federal recognition of the maturity certificate Type D in 1972. The students who select this stream often study Italian in addition to German, French, and English.

Perhaps the most significant contribution of the Federal Maturity program to relations between the linguistic groups in Switzerland is that it insures that a certain minimum standard in at least one of the national languages other than one's mother tongue is upheld by all those pursuing a higher education. Given the nature of the Swiss federal state, the establishment of fixed standards did not come easily.

Brooks (1930:184-185) observes that both the attitude toward and results of language learning in Switzerland are quite different from those prevailing in the United States:

> One is struck by the difference between Swiss nomenclature and our own on the subject. In referring to German, French, and Italian, we speak of "modern foreign languages," conveying, it is to be feared, some suggestion of the exotic or difficult, and even of inferiority, by the term "foreign." To the Swiss, one of these is his mother-tongue (*Muttersprache*, according to the federal maturity program), just as English is to us, but the other two are not foreign, instead they are second and third languages (*zweite und dritte Landessprachen*). . . . In any event, it is certain that results attained in language study put to shame not only American high schools but American colleges, universities, and graduate schools as well. . . . At 18 the young Swiss meets a maturity test involving a reading knowledge of one (or more) modern languages other than his mother-tongue. . . .

5. The core subjects are history, geography, mathematics, physics, chemistry, biology, and drawing or music.

On the primary and lower secondary level, instruction in a second or third language is a matter for cantonal regulation. Most cantons commence instruction in the second language in about the sixth or seventh year of the curriculum. Educators are divided as to whether language training should be started at a younger age. One common argument against earlier second-language training is that Swiss children must first receive a thorough instruction in their mother tongue, particularly in German Switzerland where, because of the predominance of dialect, high German has many of the characteristics of a foreign tongue. On the other hand, the Swiss Conference of Directors on Education recommended in 1976 that instruction in the second official language begin in the fourth or fifth school year (Schweizerische Konferenz der kantonalen Erziehungsdirektoren, 1976:7).

The goal of instruction in the second national language during the compulsory school years is, in the first place, to gain oral proficiency, and in the second place to achieve competence in written expression. Above all, the student should learn to understand people who speak the second language as their mother tongue and to make himself understood in normal everyday conversation (Schweizerische Konferenz, 1976:12-13). There is little doubt that Switzerland is successful in producing a large number of bilingual and plurilingual individuals at all levels of society. This can be attributed to many factors: the effectiveness of language training, individual motivation, frequent language contact, and the direct economic value of a command of modern languages.

The Role of the School Curriculum

Merriam observed in 1931 in *The Making of Citizens* that of all institutions appraised in the eight countries studied, the school plays the most important role in inculcating the population with civic values. It "emerges as the heart of the civic education of the political community and in all probability will continue to function in this role" (Merriam, 1966:344). What distinguishes the school from other institutions or activities is that it is the agency through which society makes the most deliberate attempt to shape the political outlook of its new citizens. As opposed to the family, which is essentially private, it is possible for a given regime to design and implement a fairly uniform program for the vast majority of children and adolescents in the entire society (Dawson and Prewitt, 1969:179). Through the crucial formative years, the school provides the adolescent citizen with knowledge about the political world and his or her role in it. In addition, the school transmits the consensual values and attitudes of that society.

The curriculum is potentially one of the major instruments of political socialization. It serves as an initiator and reinforcer of cultural values. As Pratt (1975:102) observes:

> For many children, textbooks constitute the bulk of the reading material that they encounter, particularly throughout the formative elementary grades. Moreover, the textbook is not simply any book, it is an official book, authorized by the government, promoted by the school, acknowledged by the teacher. Textbooks, particularly those in such social studies as history, civics, and geography, will provide students with their first introduction to many social issues. For some social and cultural questions, the influence of the textbook may remain decisive.

It is, of course, difficult to determine the influence exerted by any particular textbook. The teacher may modify or re-interpret the material contained in the text, and thus may leave in the students' minds an attitude quite different from that expressed by the author. Nevertheless, the experience from other countries shows that the majority of teachers of history and civics allow the textbook to determine to a great extent the content of instruction (Hodgetts, 1968:24, 26-27, 45).[6]

Many recent studies of school textbooks in multicultural societies have shown that they serve to divide rather than to unite the different cultural groups. Williamson (1969), in a textbook analysis of French Canadians, Indians, and Americans in authorized Ontario textbooks used from 1890 to 1930, found that although the image of the French Canadian was clearly superior to that of the Indian, it was nevertheless stereotyped. Even more striking are the results reported by Trudel and Jain (1968). Their study of a national sample of school textbooks concludes that there are substantial disagreements between Anglo and French Canadian conceptions of Canadian history. Not only do the two groups focus on different eras of Canadian history (the French Canadians on the pre-1760 period and the English Canadians on more recent events), they also attribute different and sometimes irreconcilable meanings to the same event (Trudel and Jain, 1968). Hodgetts (1968:34) concludes that:

6. Hodgetts (1968:26) notes that 87 percent of the 847 Canadian classrooms he and his coworkers observed in 1966-67 "unquestionably followed the gray, consensus version of the textbook." In a Swiss study, Altermatt and Utz (1976) also comment on the importance of the textbook in the teaching of history in Switzerland.

Canadian studies in the schools of both linguistic communities do little to encourage a mutual understanding of their separate attitudes, aspirations, and interests. Successive generations of young English- and French-speaking Canadians raised on such conflicting views of our history cannot possibly understand each other or the country in which they live.

Similar findings emerge from a study by Auerbach (1965) comparing Afrikaner and English textbooks in South Africa. He concludes that the educational system serves to divide the South African population. Significant differences were shown to exist between the presentation of history to Afrikaans-speaking and English-speaking students. Furthermore, textbooks of both language groups characterized the black Africans as inherently inferior to whites.

Thus, given the evidence from other multicultural societies we might hypothesize that Swiss textbooks would also exhibit significant differences in interpretation between the various religious and linguistic groups. In order to test this hypothesis, we shall examine a number of potentially controversial events in Swiss history.

Reading the textbooks used in the public schools is one of the best ways to gain an initial acquaintance with a foreign country (see Bierstedt, 1955:103). While school textbooks are designed primarily for the transmission of knowledge—or what is referred to as their manifest function—they serve other purposes as well. These include the latent functions of communicating the myths and the mores, the traditions and the legends, and the folkways and the superstitions which are also an integral part of the culture. A qualitative investigation[7] of potentially controversial events and recurring themes in Swiss history will enable us to shed light on both manifest and latent functions of education in transmitting interethnic sentiments.

The Selection of Swiss History Textbooks

The intense devotion to locality has been one of the outstanding characteristics of Swiss political and social life for many generations. This fact, as we have maintained previously, has given rise to a school system which, like its American and Canadian

7. See Glassner and Couzine (1979), Cicourel (1964), and Kracauer (1952) for strengths, and Berelson (1952), Cartwright (1953), and Pool (1959) for weaknesses of qualitative content analysis.

counterparts, is local rather than national in scope. Thus one is confronted with a bewildering number of school systems, each with its own curriculum, and often with its own publishing house.

Furthermore, not only national history but also local history receives considerable attention from Swiss students. In general, Swiss public schools proceed on the principle "from the near to the far" (*Vom Nahen zum Fernen*). Thus, in the lower grades the elementary student studies the home village or city, expanding to the history and customs of the county and canton, and finally, at the end of compulsory education, systematically studies Swiss and world history. This sequence is followed in most cantons. Since we are primarily interested in the treatment of Swiss national history, rather than a more local perspective, and the ways in which national and subnational alliances are treated, we shall confine our analysis to those history books used in the upper level of compulsory school (usually grades 6 through 9). These influential grades provide the last formal education received by the majority of young Swiss.

Even after narrowing the scope of the textbooks to the upper levels of secondary school, over twenty different Swiss and foreign history books were found in use during the 1975-76 school year.[8]

The final selection of ten books, six from German Switzerland and four from French Switzerland, was governed by two primary considerations. First, textbooks which were in use in more than one canton were given priority over those with a more limited audience. Secondly, an attempt was made to take into account religious, linguistic, and geographical factors.

The following is a list of the ten books which were selected, along with the cantons in which they are used.

French Textbooks

Georges-André Chevallaz, *Histoire générale de 1789 à nos jours*, 1974.

This book, which is authored by a current Federal Councillor, covers the period from 1789 to the present. It is a part of a series under the direction of the University of Lausanne. Richly illustrated, it treats, in addition to world and Swiss history, the political organization of Switzerland as a whole as well as of each

8. A questionnaire was sent out to all the cantonal departments of education between Fall 1975 and Spring 1976 in order to draw up representative lists by cantons of the textbooks used in the upper level of secondary school (*Sekundarschule Stufe* I). These lists, compiled by Dr. Hans Utz, were supplemented by additional information from the Swiss Educational Documentation Center in Geneva.

Romand canton. It is used primarily for the pre-gymnasium classes in the cantons of Vaud, Geneva, Neuchâtel, and Valais.

Henri Grandjean and Henri Jeanrenaud, *Histoire de la Suisse*, vol. 2, 1969; cited hereafter as Grandjean.

Used in the cantons of Vaud, Neuchâtel, Geneva, and Valais, this book first appeared in 1944 and was revised in 1969. It treats Swiss history from the founding of the Confederation to the present. Originally published for use in the canton of Vaud, it is representative of an older generation of textbooks used in French Switzerland.

Gérard Pfulg, *Histoire de la Suisse*, 1960.

Used in Fribourg and Valais, this book was chosen because it is typical of how Swiss history is taught in French Catholic Switzerland. It covers French history from its beginnings to the present.

Gérard Pfulg, Michael Salamin, and Maurice Zermatten, *Histoire générale*, 1974; cited hereafter as Salamin.

This book, which deals primarily with world rather than Swiss history, is used in the cantons of Valais, Fribourg, Geneva, Vaud, and Neuchâtel. Designed as a concise overview of world history for a French-speaking audience, it covers the period from antiquity to the present.

German Textbooks
Theodor Hafner, *Kurze Welt- und Schweizer-Geschichte*, 1969.

This book first appeared in 1942, was revised in 1959, and updated in 1964. Although it is currently used only as a supplementary textbook in the canton of Schwyz, it was selected because it is typical of a past generation of textbooks used in the Innerschweiz (the old Catholic cantons of German-speaking Switzerland).

Eugen Halter, *Vom Strom der Zeiten*, 1972.

Used in St. Gallen, Appenzell Inner and Outer Rhoden, Schwyz, Solothurn, Thurgau, Uri, Zug, Obwalden, and Nidwalden, this book first appeared in 1942 and was revised in 1965. Originally written for the canton of St. Gallen, it covers world and Swiss history from antiquity to the present.

Arnold Jaggi, *Von den Anfängen der Reformation bis zur Gegenwart*, 1969.

This book, which strongly bears the stamp of the canton of Bern, is also used in Thurgau, Uri, Nidwalden, and Fribourg. It first appeared in 1942 and was revised in 1969. The book covers world and Swiss history from the Reformation to the present.

Otto Müller, *Denkwürdige Vergangenheit*, vol. 1, 1968; vol. 2, 1969.
These two volumes, originating from the canton of Aargau, are also used in Bern, Basel-Land, and Schwyz. They cover world and Swiss history from antiquity to the present.

Walter Rutsch, *Welt- und Schweizergeschichte*, vol. 2, 1966.
This volume, issued by the canton of Zurich, was first published in 1952 and revised in 1963. In addition to Zurich, it is also used in Appenzell Outer Rhoden, Basel-Stadt, Schwyz, Solothurn, and Thurgau. It covers world and Swiss history from the French Revolution to the present.

Weltgeschichte im Bild, 6/1-2, 1974; 6/3, 7/1, 1975; 7/2-3, 1976; 8, 1977; 9, 1978.
This series contains eight richly illustrated booklets for grades 6 through 9, covering world and Swiss history from antiquity to the present. The Weltgeschichte im Bild series is published by the Northwestern Commission for History Instruction and authored by a team of experts with competence in the particular period of history. One important aim of these books is to coordinate the teaching of history in Aargau, Basel-Stadt, Basel-Land, Bern, Fribourg, Lucerne, and Solothurn. They are presently being used in these cantons on a trial basis.

The teaching of history and the inculcation of a political tradition which does not antagonize the two different confessions, or the three different linguistic groups, or the many different geographical sections, each with a distinct local consciousness and interest of its own, is an unusually difficult task in Switzerland. Tradition has quite frequently proved disrupting rather than unifying. Religious differences have threatened the unity of the state on more than one occasion. The home of Calvin and Zwingli, and at the same time the seat of powerful Catholic influences, Switzerland has seen the rival confessions clash repeatedly. The climax of these conflicts came in the civil war (Sonderbund War) of 1847, when geographical and religious lines coincided, with Protestants on one side and Catholics on the other. Later in the nineteenth century, reverberations from past religious conflicts occurred at the time of the *Kulturkampf*. The foundation for the increasingly intense consciousness of distinct nationality among the Jurassians was laid during this time.

Civic cohesion has also been complicated by partisan feelings among linguistic, cultural, and class groupings. The French occupation of Switzerland, at least at its onset, was received differently by the subject territories and the ruling cantons. World War I severely disrupted allegiances and threatened to split Swiss loyalties between the Central Powers and the Allies. Soon afterward, the dire conditions of the working classes and the shortages encountered during the war years precipitated a general strike in 1918.

How do Catholic and Protestant, French and German textbook writers interpret these potentially controversial events? Have they been able to overcome competing affections and allegiances? What are the themes that unite and divide the various religious, linguistic, and cultural groups? We shall turn to these and related questions in the next section.

Historical Interpretation and the Pull of Religion

All the textbook writers mention religion and its impact on history. However, the different authors give varying interpretations of events such as the Reformation, the Sonderbund War, and the *Kulturkampf*, where religion has played a decisive role. In the 1920s Robert Brooks (1930:183) observed that "in Catholic cantons, both priesthood and laity stand aghast constantly at the 'false teachings' about the Middle Ages and the Reformation tolerated in the schools of Protestant cantons; and of course the same feeling reversed exists among the followers of Zwingli and Calvin" (see also the Swiss National Commission for UNESCO, 1957:10-11). Does the cleavage in interpretation still persist?

At first glance, it appears that most Swiss authors cite the same events and conditions as sparking the Reformation in Europe. The most commonly cited reasons are the schism in the church, with as many as three popes at the same time proclaiming to be the spiritual leader; secularization of the clergy; and the selling of indulgences. On closer examination, however, we find that differences in nuances and interpretations do appear. The most pervasive differences are found between Protestant and Catholic books. The Catholic authors cite humanism as an important cause of the Reformation, criticizing it in no uncertain terms:

> Among the causes (of the Reformation) is humanism. Its followers took great care to live a good life. However, they did not organize it any longer with a view toward the afterlife. Furthermore, they believed that the human mind would be strong enough to guide its own way, without being directed by the Church. They considered the

ministry of the Church unnecessary and worthless. They despised the uneducated clergy and did not want to follow them. (Hafner:123)[9] The Renaissance in humanities and the arts led to a real return to paganism in morals. Certain humanists were so enthusiastic about the works of antiquity that they strayed from Christianity. (Pfulg: 167; see also Salamin:151)[10]

In addition, both the German and French Catholic books condemn questioning the Church doctrine as weakening the faith (Pfulg:167; Salamin:151; Hafner:124-125). For Hafner, this is a recurring theme. He pictures Calvin and Zwingli, the two Swiss reformers, as pious men who lost their way amid attempts to reform the Church (Hafner:124-125). Pfulg and Salamin rarely lapse into such orthodox interpretations (see Table 6). Pfulg is the only author who speculates that the Reformation, although it dissolved the religious unity of Switzerland, may have had the unexpected consequence of making it capable of surviving as an entity over the centuries. He observes that after being converted to Protestantism, Vaud was able to break the hold of the Savoyan empire. Thus by effectively becoming bilingual with the incorporation of French-speaking areas, Switzerland may later have been able to resist the nationalistic movements (pan-Germanism and irredentism) of the nineteenth century (Pfulg:179).

In contrast with the Catholic books, those originating from the old Protestant cantons tend to take a more favorable stance toward the Reformation. As we might expect, they fill in the details leading up to the Reformation with anticipation, whereas the Catholic books introduce it with regret. The French Catholic writer Salamin, for example, observes that with the conversion of Bern the balance was tilted in favor of the Protestants. From then on the two camps violently clashed with one another, dividing the unity of Switzerland for a long time before a compromise was finally reached (Salamin:154-155). The German Protestant author, Jaggi, on the other hand, spends a considerable amount of time glorifying the new belief. According to his interpretation,

9. Dazu ist der Humanismus zu rechnen. Seine Anhänger legten alle Sorgfalt darauf, hienieden ein schönes (menschenwürdiges) Leben zu leben, ordneten es aber nicht mehr auf ein Jenseits hin. Auch glaubten sie, dass der menschliche Geist stark genug sei, sich selber zurechtzufinden, ohne dass ihm der Weg durch eine Kirche gewiesen würde. Das kirchliche Lehramt dünkte sie überflüssig und unwürdig. Sie verachteten den ungebildeten Klerus und wollten von ihm nichts annehmen.

10. La renaissance des lettres et des arts a amené dans les moeurs un véritable retour au paganisme. Certains humanistes s'enthousiasment à tel point pour les oeuvres de l'antiquité, qu'ils en arrivent à se détacher du christianisme.

TABLE 6. Treatment of important figures in Swiss history

	Calvin	Zwingli	Napoleon
Chevallaz	Not covered	Not covered	*Had natural authority. *Military genius. *Re-established order. *Provided civil code and developed public education. *Didn't hesitate to put down opposition. *Normalized relations with Catholic Church. *Guaranteed religious freedom. *Used church and school to help him keep order. (pp. 46-62)
Grandjean	*Greatest reformer of French origin. *Among the great French writers of his time. *Imposed strict rules of conduct. *Fought against those who criticized his doctrine and finally triumphed. *Founded academy to consolidate his teachings. *Gave Geneva European reputation. (pp. 99-102)	*Principal reformer in German Switzerland. *Relied only on text of Bible. *Strong adversary of mercenary and pension system. *Defended views in public discussion. *Preached against indulgences. *Supported by city council. *Banned monasteries and replaced them with schools and hospitals. (pp. 82-83)	*Mediator and reorganizer of Switzerland. *Imposed Act of Mediation, which was favorably received by most of the cantons. *Secured ten years of progress in education and engineering feats. *Forced Switzerland into military agreement with France. (pp. 151-156)

Ochs	La Harpe	Dufour
*Favored French intervention, out of vanity and out of revolutionary conviction. *Instrumental in drafting Helvetic Constitution. *One of principal magistrates of the city of Basel. (p. 71)	*Talented advocate. *Teacher of Russian czar. *Animator of Helvetic club. *Petitioned France to intervene to free Vaudois people. *Demonstrated collusion between Swiss aristocrats and royalists. *Drew attention to Bernese treasury. *Demanded Vaud become French protectorate until it could be annexed by grand Republic. (p. 71)	*Free of partisan passion. *Conducted campaign with speed and moderation and with little loss of blood. (p. 133)
*Emissary of Basel government to Paris. *Favored reorganization of Switzerland. *Like La Harpe, favored French intervention. *Gave Napoleon pretext for intervention. (p. 142)	*Banned by rulers of Bern. *Worked for independence of home country (Vaud), and to throw off yoke of Bernese rule. *Asked France to take Vaud under its protection. (p. 142)	*Officer in Napoleon's army. *Helped organize federal army. *Made maps of Switzerland. *Conscious of responsibility. *Led the war quickly and with humanity. (p. 176)

TABLE 6 cont.

	Calvin	Zwingli	Napoleon
Pfulg	*Very strict in matters of faith and morals. *Condemned critics of his doctrine. *Under Calvin, Geneva became the Protestant Rome. *Founded academy to consolidate his works. (p. 177)	*Declared enemy of mercenary and pension system. *Gave personal interpretation of the Bible. *Only considered institutions of early church as valid. *Defended ideas in public discussions. *Warlike. (pp. 170-172)	*Initiator of great works. *Considerable progress made during ten peaceful years of Napoleonic rule, especially in education, and engineering feats. *Ruined Swiss industry for the benefit of France. *Swiss had to provide soldiers. (pp. 242-248)
Salamin	*Adhered to doctrines of Luther when young. *Later developed own ideas, especially doctrine of predestination. *Governed as absolute ruler in Geneva for 25 years. *Did not tolerate any opposition. (pp. 155-156)	*Introduced Reformation into Switzerland. (pp. 154-155)	*Genius went beyond military domain. *Great statesman of varied interests. *Profoundly marked life of French nation and Europe. *Man of unlimited ambition. *Instituted universal suffrage, but this remained a fiction. *Numerous achievements: education, arrangement with church, civil code. *Under him liberal spirit prospered. (pp. 212-223)

Ochs	La Harpe	Dufour
*Ochs and La Harpe mentioned together as prime collaborators of French propagandists in Switzerland. *Demanded French support for Vaudois independence. *They gave France the pretext for invading Switzerland. (p. 237)		*Campaign carried out with speed and humanity. *Author of several works on military subjects. *Masterwork was map of Switzerland. (pp. 263, 273)
---	*Not mentioned by name; French army entered Vaud, called in by some Vaudois. (p. 211)	---

TABLE 6 cont.

	Calvin	Zwingli	Napoleon
Hafner	*Sharp mind and strong will. *Ascetic way of life. *Signed 58 death penalties and 76 bannings. *Saw primarily evil in the world. *Believed in predestination. *Wanted to make Geneva into a theocracy. *Founded academy to educate ministers. *Made life-loving Genevans into serious, hard-working, economically successful people. (p. 127)	*Well-educated humanist. *Good orator. *Explained Holy Scriptures rationally. *Questioned "mysteries" of Catholic Church. *At first worked in good faith against abuses within the Church, then went too far. *Abolished mass, considered Bible as exclusive source of faith. *Wanted to spread his faith with means and might of the state. (p. 126)	*One of the greatest military leaders of all time. *Would have been one of the greatest statesmen, had he been more moderate and not abused the people as a tool of his ambition. *Goal was to make France a big power in Europe. *Died in St. Helena as a repentent son of the Church. (pp. 155-158)
Halter	*Introduced rigid rules for the city and church. *Made Geneva into a state of God. *When he died, left behind a citizenry ready to sacrifice everything for their faith and their city. *Founded academy for educating ministers. (pp. 26-28)	*Humanist background. *Passionate adversary of mercenary service. *Against indulgences. *Considered Bible as only source of faith. *Tried to spread his new faith with arms. (pp. 20-24)	*Superior military leader. *Introduced strict central regime and civil code. *Made agreement with Pope. *Extraordinarily hard-working man. *Power-hungry. *Wanted weak confederation in the interest of France. (pp. 66-90)

Ochs	La Harpe	Dufour
*Rulers in Paris commissioned him to write the constitution for "liberated Switzerland." *Patterned Helvetic Constitution on French example. (p. 162)	*Educator of Russian Czar. *One of the main enemies of aristocrats in Paris. *Called for fight against Bernese government. (p. 159)	*Noble and moderate, but that cannot be said to the same extent about his troops. (pp. 173-174)
*Spent youth abroad and received French education. *Man of the world who quickly received high office. *Wanted to renew Switzerland. *By keeping good relations with French government, made intervention easier. *Wrote Helvetic Constitution based on French example. *Collaborator with French government. (pp. 69-75)	*Banned by Bernese. *Wanted to free Vaud from Bernese rule and make it equal part of Switzerland. *Hatred for Bernese had no limits. *Blinded by promise of French revolutionaries. *Asked French to intervene and free Vaud. *Collaborator with French government. (p. 69)	*Noble-thinking Genevan. *Managed to lead campaign almost without loss of blood. (p. 108)

TABLE 6 cont.

	Calvin	Zwingli	Napoleon
Jaggi	*Hard worker. *Believed in predestination. *Introduced rigid rules in Geneva. *Ruled Geneva according to his own will; many dissenters were executed or exiled. *Founded academy. *Bern arranged a safe refuge for Calvin in Geneva, thereby exerting a powerful influence on world history. (pp. 64-69)	*Very pious man. *Occupied himself with concerns of fatherland. *Took strong stand against mercenary service. *Recommended strict neutrality. *Good orator. *Questioned authority of church. *Believed in Bible as only source of faith. *Proclaimed as heretic by detractors. *Defended views in public. (pp. 33-41)	*Clever, sharp-willed, and power-hungry. *Extraordinary military talent. *Removed privileges so that everyone was equal before the judge and tax collector. *Because of him, Swiss experienced meaning of foreign occupation. *Erred in thinking people liked to speak of freedom but in reality would be indifferent. *Perhaps lesson of violence served to awaken the desire for freedom. (pp. 158-176)
Müller	*Most influential reformer after Luther. *Believed in predestination. *After original sin, thought nothing good left in man. *Considered Bible as only true foundation of faith. *Instituted austere life in Geneva. *Punished those disagreeing with him. *Fought for glory of God. (Vol. 1, pp. 193-196)	*Teachings dependent on Bible alone. *Against mercenary service. *Intransigent, did not want to stop before his faith was spread everywhere. (Vol. 1, pp. 187-190)	*Ambitious and gifted ruler who took reins of state tightly in his hands. *Warlike. *People had equality before the law, but no sovereignty. *Used church as tool. *Limited equal rights and freedom when they stood in the way of his power. *Instituted civil code. *Independent and tyrannical. *Died bitter and lonely. (Vol. 2, pp. 23-33)

Ochs	La Harpe	Dufour
*Born into aristocratic Baseler family. *Spent many of his early years abroad. *Didn't learn Swiss German (dialect). *Was very ambitious, hard-working, and shrewd. *Quickly obtained a high position in Basel. *Was of weak character. *Ardent follower of the Enlightenment. *Rejoiced at the coming of the French Revolution. *Advised Napoleon to invade Switzerland. *Wrote Napoleon that he was delighted about the invasion of Munster and St. Imier. (pp. 202-203, 226)	*Passionate, behaved similarly to character-weak Ochs. *Hated the Bernese. *Attempted to incite Vaudois through pamphlets. (p. 203)	*Fought for the security and embellishment of his home city. *Also served ardently all of the fatherland. *Reluctantly became general of Confederate army. *Handled war with speed and moderation. *Because of him, losses were low. *Proud, he wasn't resented by Sonderbund cantons. *Many smoked pipes, called "Dufourli," that had his picture on them. *Made maps of Switzerland. (pp. 279-281)
*Told Napoleon revolution could only come about with French help. *Claimed France would be endangered until Switzerland was revolutionized. (Vol. 2, p. 35)	*Intransigence of Swiss government to introduction of any reforms led La Harpe and Ochs to ask the French to put pressure on Switzerland and invade if necessary. (Vol. 2, p. 35)	*Carried out war with speed and little loss of life. *Soldiers committed violent acts despite his warning. *Showed a conciliatory attitude and humanity. *Even citizens of Sonderbund cantons smoked pipes, called "Dufourli," that had his picture on them. (Vol. 2, pp. 69-70)

TABLE 6 cont.

	Calvin	Zwingli	Napoleon
Rutsch	Not covered.	Not covered.	*Ambitious, self-righteous, efficient, and autocratic. *In fairy-tale manner, rose to power and glory. *Instituted civil code. *Conserved unity of France and equality of the citizens. *French had to sacrifice their freedom in exchange for law and order. *Time of Napoleon meant time of war. (pp. 22-36)
Weltgeschichte im Bild	*Didn't tolerate opposition. *Made Geneva theocracy; it became known as the reformed Rome. *Hard worker. *Thought God not impressed by good work or by honest faith. *Believed in predestination. *Very strict and austere. *Took in refugees who supported his political position. (7/2, pp. 27-29)	*Always felt like Confederate and loved Confederation. *Scholar of humanism. *As army chaplain, was against mercenary service. *Defended and spread his faith by arms. (7/2, pp. 38-40)	*Skilled military leader. *Very ambitious. *Was intelligent enough to keep the most important reforms of the Revolution. *Came to an agreement with Catholic Church. *Civil code was one of main achievements. *Gave Switzerland Act of Mediation. *Had good knowledge of Swiss circumstances. (8, pp. 25-28, 94)

Ochs	La Harpe	DuFour
*Enthusiastic follower of Enlightenment and French Revolution. *Despised "run-down" Confederation. *Like La Harpe, thought of revolution with French help. *Overstepped his authority when Napoleon gave him the task of writing a new constitution. *Like La Harpe, became a traitor to his country. *Vain and felt he was involved in important event. (p. 43)	*Of noble birth, educated. *A Vaudois who didn't like Bern. *Educator of the Czar. *Wrote letters to the Directorate, often exaggerating the harshness of Bernese oppression. *Passionate love of Vaud made him a traitor to the Confederation. (p. 42)	*Reluctantly took responsibility of commanding Federal troops. *Moderate and humane. *Diet could not have made better choice. *Led war with speed and little loss of life. *His map of Switzerland an important achievement. (pp. 100-102)
*Spent youth abroad. *At first a member of "Patriots" who wanted to bring about revolution without French help; then came under the influence of Napoleon. *Drafted Helvetic Constitution. *Didn't realize that he would only be a tool of Napoleon. *Made first member of Helvetic Senate. (8, p. 95)	*Educator of the Czar. *Fought for liberation of Vaud from Bern. *Invited French to invade Vaud. *At Viennese Congress, used good relations with Russia to win over the Czar to recognize Swiss independence (8, p. 95)	*Led war with moderation and speed and little loss of life. *Decided reluctantly to take over command. (8, p. 102)

even the "inhabitants of the villages surrounding Bern listened to the new teachings with eagerness, and thought about them while plowing and scattering the seeds" (Jaggi:42).

While most authors, both French and German, Protestant and Catholic, give a fairly objective picture of Calvin and Zwingli, differences also emerge among the various Swiss textbooks (see Table 6). Two German books, but none of the French books, note that Zwingli was a loyal Swiss patriot who loved his fatherland and occupied himself with the concerns of the Confederation (Weltgeschichte im Bild, 7/2:38; Jaggi:33). The French Protestant author Grandjean (p. 102) praises the accomplishments of Calvin, classifying him as one of the greatest writers of his time in the French language. On the other hand, the Catholic authors (especially Hafner) give a more reserved portrait of these two men.

In spite of their varying interpretations of the events and ideas connected with the Reformation, the textbook authors seem to agree that the true Swiss way should be through compromise and mediation of differences. The image of the two opposing sides sharing a milk soup after the truce of the first *Kappel* War, with the Catholic Innerschweizers supplying the milk and the Protestant Zurichers providing the bread, is referred to (and illustrated) in almost all of the textbooks (Müller, vol. 1:191; Jaggi:52-54; Weltgeschichte im Bild, 7/2:41; Halter:23; Hafner:129; Grandjean:244; Pfulg:172). It is noteworthy that this, rather than the wars of religion—which are often given only cursory treatment in the textbooks—has been passed down as part of the Swiss tradition. The mediator, particularly in the German language books, is an important part of the cultural heritage of Switzerland. Hafner (p. 129) emphasizes this spirit by noting the "role of a true Confederate" played in Solothurn by Nikolaus Wengli, as well as referring to the successful mediation of the Glarner Landamann Aebli. Likewise, Müller (vol. 1:191) refers to this event as "an unforgettable picture of true Confederate compatibility" (see also Halter:23; Jaggi:54-55).

The rivalry between the two confessions climaxed in 1847 with the Sonderbund War. In many respects it was a war of religion, with the dominant Protestant group taking the side of nationalism, and the Catholics that of localism. The German textbooks from two Protestant cantons, Bern and Zurich, tie the conflict specifically to the issue of whether the Confederation should have a new constitution (Rutsch:98; Jaggi:285). The cantons desiring a new, more liberal constitution and those hoping to keep the Pact of 1815 coincided with Protestant and Catholic cantons, respectively. This cleavage between liberal Protestants and conservative Catholics, according to the German Catholic author Hafner (p. 172), made Switzerland more polarized along religious lines than other countries are.

While almost all the books agree that both sides aggravated the rift between Catholic and Protestant cantons (Halter:106; Chevallaz:130; Pfulg:262; Weltgeschichte im Bild, 7/2:100), two German-language authors try either to find excuses for their own side or to tell only part of the story. Jaggi denounces the action of the Freischarenzüge (the radical volunteer groups which retaliated against the conservatives in the canton of Lucerne), but at the same time tries to find excuses for them. "In spite of this, a wise conservative assures us that there were very valiant men among the Freischärlern. Many honestly believed that they were performing a duty for their fatherland"[11] (Jaggi:276).

The bias in the Hafner book, on the other hand, is more subtle. It correctly traces the increased tensions between Catholic and Protestant cantons to the abolishment of the monasteries in Aargau, which it notes violated the Pact of 1815. However, it fails to point out that calling in the Jesuits in Lucerne, while it was not unlawful, also served to polarize the situation. Neither Hafner nor Pfulg acknowledges that by seeking help from abroad, the Sonderbund (a defensive pact created by the Catholic cantons of Lucerne, Uri, Schwyz, Unterwalden, Zug, Fribourg, and Valais) violated the Federal Pact.

General Dufour, the commander of the Confederate troops, is mentioned in all of the textbooks covering Swiss history (see Table 6). As might be expected, the textbook authors from the Protestant cantons which stayed loyal to the Confederation are unified in their praise of Dufour, whom they variously describe as a man "devoid of partisan passion" (Chevallaz:133) and "conscious of his responsibility" (Grandjean:176). Rutsch (p. 100) notes that the Diet could not have made a better choice. Many of the books quote Dufour's famous speech in which he appealed to his troops to spare the civil population of the enemy (Jaggi:283; Halter:108; Müller, vol. 2:69; Rutsch:102; Weltgeschichte im Bild, 8:102; Grandjean:253).

Even the books from the Sonderbund cantons, which might be expected to glorify General von Salis-Soglio, the commander of the Sonderbund troops, commend the merits of Dufour. Hafner,

---

11. Und doch gab es unter den Freischärlern, so versichert ein kluger Konservativer, "sehr wackere Männer und Jünglinge. Viele glaubten redlich, eine Pflicht gegen ihr Vaterland zu erfüllen."

a German Catholic author, comments (p. 174) that General Dufour "proved himself to be moderate in carrying out his duty, which cannot be said to the same extent for his troops."[12] Pfulg's book, used in the French Catholic cantons of Fribourg and Valais, observes, like many texts used in the old federal cantons, that Dufour conducted the war rapidly and with humanity (Pfulg:263; Grandjean:176; Müller, vol. 2:70; Jaggi:281, 284; Halter:109; Chevallaz:133; Weltgeschichte im Bild, 8:102-103).

The Constitution of 1848 is heralded by the textbook writers from the Protestant cantons of German and French Switzerland as a diplomatic work of major proportions. Many authors contrast it with the overcentralized regime of the Helvetic period and the loose alliance of states characterized by the Pact of 1815:

> It combined in a most favorable way the old and the new tendencies. All the cantons and half-cantons remained independent states with their own government, even though they had to give up a part of their former sovereignty. (Müller, vol. 2:71)[13]

> Both major parties helped in the framing of the Constitution for the new Swiss state. The Liberals wanted a strong Confederation, the Conservatives, strong cantons. The new Confederation is a compromise between the two. (Halter:111)[14]

> This Constitution, the result of a compromise between different tendencies, has proven to be a good work! It is the foundation of modern Switzerland. Thanks to the institutions introduced in 1848, our country has not only been able to enjoy peace in the middle of turmoil, but has also enjoyed considerable progress. (Grandjean: 179)[15]

In the two Catholic books, opposition is voiced to some aspects of the new Constitution; Hafner (p. 175) and Pfulg (p. 264) observe that the Liberals showed their dislike of the Jesuits by banning them and forbidding the founding of new monasteries. Pfulg (p.

12. . . . hatte sich bei der Durchführung seiner Aufgabe hervorragend edel und gemässigt gezeigt, was von den Truppen selbst nicht im gleichen Masse behauptet werden kann.

13. Sie verband in glücklichster Weise die alten und die neuen Anliegen. Alle Kantone und Halbkantone blieben selbständige Staaten mit eigener Regierung, wenn sie auch einen Teil ihrer bisherigen Machtbefugnisse abtreten mussten.

14. Beim Neubau der Schweiz haben beide grossen Parteien mitgeholfen. Die Liberalen wollten einen starken Bund, die Konservativen starke Kantone: Der neue Bund ist die Lösung der Mitte.

15. Cette constitution, résultat d'un compromis entre des tendences diverses, s'est révélée une oeuvre bonne. Elle a crée la Suisse contemporaine et, grâce aux institutions nées de 1848, notre patrie a pu non seulement jouir de la paix au milieu des tourmentes, mais encore faire de réel progrès.

264) also adds that the Constitution of 1848 sanctioned the victory of 1847, leaving the radicals in absolute control of the politics of the Confederation. Nevertheless, the two Catholic authors' overall assessment is one of praise:

> The Constitution of 1848 represented a compromise between the overly loose association of pre-revolutionary times, the Mediation, and the Pact of 1815, on one hand, and the overly rigid organization of the Helvetic period. It allowed the individual cantons, in spite of the unification of the country, to live a life suited to their own special situation. (Hafner:175)[16]

> The Constitution of 1848 represents an important step toward democracy. . . . It favors centralization, however, without rejecting federalism, which in our country is in accord with our nature and our traditions. (Pfulg:275)[17]

Chevallaz (p. 203; see also Jaggi:288) adds that the Constitution of 1848 is of special importance because, unlike the Helvetic Constitution of 1798 and the Act of Mediation of 1803, which were imposed by France, and the Pact of 1815, which was established under the control of foreign powers: "The Constitution of 1848—worked out at a time when Europe was in a state of turmoil—was drafted and adopted in complete independence."[18]

Despite the fact that the textbook authors put forth different interpretations of the events surrounding the Sonderbund War, they agree that the new Constitution provided a harmonization between new and old tendencies. Liberals and Conservatives cooperated, and in the end were successful in molding modern Switzerland. The Confederation was transformed by her own will. Her nationhood was not based on language, religion, or culture, but on general consent to a federalistic and democratic order.

Religion again became a vital point of contention during the time of the *Kulturkampf*. The struggle between Liberals and Conservatives broke out in Europe following the declaration of papal infallibility in 1870. Interestingly, the repercussions of this event in Switzerland are only discussed by the two Catholic authors.

16. Die Verfassung von 1848 stellte einen Ausgleich dar zwischen dem allzu lockeren Staatenbunde der Vorrevolutionszeit, der Mediation und dem 1815er— Vertrag einerseits und dem allzu straffen Bundesstaat der Helvetik anderseits. Er ermöglichte den einzelnen Kantonen der vielgestaltigen Schweiz, trotz der Einheit ein ihren Verhältnissen angepasstes Sonderleben zu führen.

17. La constitution de 1848 marque un progrès sensible vers la démocratie. . . . La constitution de 1848 favorise la centralisation, sans toutefois rejeter le fédéralisme qui, chez nous, est conforme à la nature des choses et à la tradition.

18. La Constitution de 1848 élaborée en un moment où toute l'Europe était en effervescence, fut délibérée et adoptée en toute indépendance.

They point out that the Church was seen as jeopardizing progress (Pfulg:276; Hafner:183, 184). "The Catholics are represented as being the enemies of civilization; one accuses them of being blindly attached to the holy seat, one starts to doubt their patriotism" (Pfulg:276).[19]

These two textbook authors, however, emphasize different aspects of this movement. The French author, Pfulg, stresses the political repercussions of the *Kulturkampf*, noting that its excesses in Switzerland led to a sudden change to a conservative government in Lucerne and in the Ticino. While there was a clear majority in Lucerne, in the Ticino the conservatives had to resort to gerrymandering the districts in order to come to power. Unable to regain power within legal means, the liberals resorted to a coup d'état. Intervention of the army was necessary to maintain order, and peace was restored only after both parties agreed to institute the proportional system for electing the cantonal parliament.

Pfulg further notes that the bishops of Basel and Geneva were exiled, and that the clergy were expelled from their churches in Geneva and the Bernese Jura. Fortunately, the disastrous effects of this struggle were of short duration. An outward sign of the rapprochement between liberals and conservatives was the election of Joseph Zemp, a well-known Catholic leader, to the Federal Council in 1891 (Pfulg:277-278).

The German Catholic author Hafner, on the other hand, in his short discussion of the *Kulturkampf*, concentrates on religious rather than political developments. He comments (p. 20) that those who held true to the Pope were persecuted in many countries (Germany, Italy, France, and Switzerland):

> Monasteries were abolished, religious orders were banned, worshipping was made difficult or impossible for the faithful. The *Kulturkampf* in Switzerland was most violent in the Bernese Jura and in Geneva.[20]

Evidently the events connected with the *Kulturkampf* linger only in the memory of Catholic Switzerland. A few of the Protestant textbooks fleetingly mention it with reference to Germany (Che-

19. Les catholiques sont présentés comme des ennemis de la civilisation; on leur reproche un attachement aveugle au Saint-Siège, on se met à douter de leur patriotisme.

20. Der Verlauf war fast überall derselbe: Missliebige Bischöfe wurden ins Gefängnis geworfen, die Priesterausbildungsanstalten (Seminarien) unter die Aufsicht des Staates gestellt, das Vermögen der Kirchen und kirchlichen Stiftungen eingezogen, die Klöster aufgehoben, die Orden verboten, den Gläubigen der Gottesdienst erschwert und verunmöglicht. In der Schweiz verlief dieser Kulturkampf am heftigsten im Berner Jura und in Genf.

vallaz:214, Weltgeschichte im Bild, 8:46); however, it is totally ignored in the Swiss context. Its omission from the Bernese textbook by Jaggi, which devotes a considerable amount of space to specifically Bernese history, is particularly conspicuous. The *Kulturkampf* left a heritage of bitter memories in the northern Catholic districts of the Jura, which have been the center of most separatist activity.

Historical Interpretation, Partisan Feelings, and the Attraction of Language and Culture

The pull of language and culture, like religion, may appear in various interpretations of events. Although, historically, religious differences have almost always been more serious than linguistic ones, the Swiss have on occasion also been responsive to various emotional appeals of nationalism emanating from their neighbors. Competing linguistic and geographical loyalties surfaced during, and after, the French occupation of Switzerland. Thus one might expect interpretations of this event in textbooks of the German-speaking cantons, which lost subject territories and a share of their power and prestige, to differ from those in textbooks used in the French cantons, especially Vaud, Geneva, and Neuchâtel, which were subject territories and gained the status of full cantons after the Napoleonic intervention.

This does not appear to be the case. Instead, the shared struggles against a common foe have served the purpose of articulating the fundamental underpinnings of Swiss democracy. The Helvetic Constitution is used as a concrete example of the unsuitability of the centralized regime for Switzerland's diverse peoples (Grandjean:151; Pfulg:242; Hafner:164; Halter:75; Jaggi:225-226). Grandjean notes (p. 151) that "The new regime did not suit Switzerland, which was too diverse to be unified."[21] This sentiment is also echoed in the textbooks from German Switzerland:

> The new Constitution was indeed an artificial, shoddy work which was completely unsuitable for our country and our people. It created a strictly centralized state with a large state bureaucracy. (Halter: 75)[22]

21. Le régime nouveau ne convenait pas à la Suisse, trop diverse pour être unifiée.

22. Die neue Verfassung war in der Tat ein künstliches Machwerk, das für unser Land und Volk gar nicht passte. Sie schuf einen straffen Einheitsstaat mit einer starken Zentralregierung und einem grossen Beamtenapparat.

Its lesson that a centralized state is not suitable for our people with such diverse backgrounds has not been forgotten. The time of the Helvetic will furthermore serve to remind us, forever, how much misery the foreign occupation brought to our land. (Jaggi:225-226)[23]

In addition, textbooks from both language communities and religious groups stress that one of the adverse effects of the French occupation of Switzerland was the loss of her traditional neutrality and independence. Napoleon imposed upon Switzerland a neutrality favorable to France. He demanded that the Swiss supply 16,000 soldiers for his army, and imposed a continental blockade which was to the disadvantage of Switzerland's young industries (Hafner:165; Halter:81; Jaggi:231; Müller, vol. 2:58; Rutsch:66, 70; Pfulg:241, 247; Grandjean:150, 155; Chevallaz:78, 121).

Under the Helvetic Republic and the Mediation, Switzerland did not have her free will: She was a vassal of France, and her neutrality—recognized by Napoleon—was no more than theory. (Chevallaz:121)[24]

Although Switzerland enjoyed ten years of peace and freedom amidst a war-torn Europe, thanks to the French emperor, the Swiss auxiliary troops suffered heavy casualties on the battlefields and the continental blockade was very damaging to Switzerland. More serious, however, was the fact that our country was dependent on France. For fifteen years Switzerland had to give up her traditional neutrality. Only after the downfall of Napoleon was she again able to determine her own fate. (Rutsch:70)[25]

The French-language authors observe that the Mediation period from 1803 to 1813, despite its drawbacks, secured for Switzerland ten years of relative tranquility, during which time considerable progress was made. Public education was furthered by Pestalozzi and Father Girard. A route over the Simplon was com-

23. Ihre Lehre aber, dass der Einheitsstaat für unser vielstämmiges Volk nicht passt, haben wir nicht vergessen. Die Zeit der Helvetik soll uns auch für immer daran erinnern, was die Fremdherrschaft für Leid und Elend über das Land gebracht hat.

24. Sous l'Helvétique et sous la Médiation, la Suisse n'était pas libre de choisir: Elle était vassale de la France et sa neutralité—reconnue par Napoléon—n'était qu'une formule théorique.

25. Wohl hatte die Schweiz dem französichen Kaiser ein Jahrzehnt der Ruhe und des Friedens inmitten eines von Kriegen zerrissenen Europas zu verdanken gehabt. Aber die Schweizer Hilfstruppen hatten auf den Schlachtfeldern grosse Verluste erlitten, und die Kontinentalsperre hatte der Schweiz schweren Schaden zugefügt. Bedenklicher aber war der Umstand, dass unser Land von Frankreich abhängig gewesen war. Für anderthalb Jahrzehnte hatte die Schweiz ihre traditionelle Neutralität aufgeben müssen. Erst nach dem Sturze Napoleons bot sich die Gelegenheit, das Schicksal wieder selbst zu bestimmen.

pleted, and the Linth Canal was built to connect the Lake of Zurich and Lake of Walen (Pfulg:247; Grandjean:154). Chevallaz points out (p. 78) that the new cantons served a useful apprenticeship as sovereign cantons; furthermore, in Vaud feudal privileges were suppressed, a cantonal hospital was built, and penal and civil codes of law were drafted.

The German-language authors, on the other hand, stress the price at which this freedom and tranquility was bought. They tend to see this period as one of hardship rather than one of great progress. Halter (p. 83), for example, discusses the engineering feat of the Linth Canal and its architect, Hans Konrad Escher, under the subtitle "A true patriot in a difficult time."

While the textbooks cover a fairly wide spectrum of opinion, none of the authors go so far as to praise Peter Ochs and César Frédéric La Harpe, the two Swiss who were instrumental in ushering in the Helvetic Republic (see Table 6). Most critical is the view expressed by the German Swiss Bernese author Jaggi, who condemns Ochs and La Harpe for being weak in character. He even infers (pp. 202-203) that Ochs could hardly be considered a true Swiss. In addition, writers of both language communities accuse Ochs of overambitiousness and vanity. Chevallaz (p. 71) observes that in spite of his high offices in Basel and his considerable fortune, he favored the intervention of France out of personal ambition as well as out of revolutionary conviction. La Harpe is also looked upon as a traitor to the Confederation. However, some of the books note that this was the unfortunate consequence of his deep loyalty to Vaud, his homeland (Weltgeschichte im Bild, 8:95; Rutsch:42; Halter:69; Chevallaz:71).

Napoleon Bonaparte, the main figure dealt with during this period, receives a mixed treatment in the Swiss textbooks (see Table 6). Pfulg and Grandjean, the two French-language authors who cover only Swiss history, give a factual account of his leadership during the French occupation in Switzerland, but refrain from further comment (Grandjean:151-157; Pfulg:245-247). In contrast, Chevallaz and Salamin, who assign a greater amount of space to world than to national history, point to Napoleon's military genius and to reforms in the wider civil sphere, such as the civil code and improvements in the educational system (Chevallaz: 46-50; Salamin:212-217). While the German-speaking authors also point to the military genius of Napoleon, as well as to some of his civil accomplishments, consistent with their interpretation of the French occupation of Switzerland, they connect his name with widespread plundering and war, and the loss of independence

(Hafner:155-158; Halter:66-68; Jaggi:158-176; Müller, vol. 2:23-33; Rutsch:23-36).

The most critical period for Swiss national unity came during the early years of the twentieth century. With the outbreak of World War I in 1914, both French and German Swiss felt the pull of conflicting nationalisms toward their respective cultural kin. Thus it is significant that only half of the textbooks, three German-Swiss and two French-Swiss books, mention the *Graben* or *Fossé* between the language groups. All five observe that the outbreak of the war found Switzerland deeply divided, with the German Swiss in sympathy with the German cause and the French Swiss aligned with the French (Müller, vol. 2:148; Rutsch:238; Weltgeschichte im Bild, 9:91; Chevallaz:420; Pfulg:290).

Pfulg (p. 297) maintains that the German Swiss changed their mind in favor of the Allies with the invasion of Belgium, the burning of Louvain, and the destruction of Ypres. Chevallaz (p. 420), on the other hand, singles out the "affaire des colonels" and the Hoffmann affair as provoking the gulf between the two language communities. He observes that two colonels regularly supplied the German military attaché with the army bulletin. To the dismay of the French Swiss, these two officers were given very light sentences. A Federal Councillor (Chevallaz does not use Hoffmann's name) tried privately to arrange a separate peace between the Soviet Union and Germany, and had to resign over this breach of neutrality.

The German-speaking authors of Weltgeschichte im Bild (9:91-92) also mention the Hoffmann affair—but, unlike Chevallaz, they do not tie it directly to the gulf between French and German Swiss. The other German authors covering this event, Müller and Rutsch, do not relate the above details, but rather use this incident as a vehicle for stressing that fellowship (*Brüderschaft*) between Confederates should be regarded more highly than friendship with one's cultural kin. In this context they (Müller, vol. 2:148; Rutsch, 239), along with the authors of Weltgeschichte im Bild (9:91), quote the memorable speech delivered by the Swiss poet Carl Spitteler during the war:

> We must realize that our political brother is closer to us than the best neighbor and racial kin. No one should depend on the friendship that exists between us and a neighboring people in times of peace. Before a military command and the patriotic clang of the war trumpet, all other sounds die down, even the voice of friendship. In spite of seeming intimacy, which makes us feel at home because of our common language, we must not take a different position toward the

German Empire than toward any other state—the position of reserved neutrality. Then we take the right, the neutral, the Swiss
standpoint.[26]

It is noteworthy, and perhaps characteristic of Swiss textbooks as a whole, that they stress topics of general agreement
rather than of dissent. For example, rather than speaking about
the gulf between the two language groups, they stress the hard-
ships of war and the role played by the Swiss Red Cross and other
organizations in aiding war victims (Grandjean:213-215; Pfulg:
297-298; Jaggi:355-356; Hafner:204; Weltgeschichte im Bild, 9:91).
The General Strike of 1918 is likewise treated in a conciliatory
way. Almost half of the Swiss textbooks treat it in a few sentences (Hafner, Müller) or ignore it altogether (Jaggi, Grandjean).
How, asks one critic, can the students understand the peace agreement between workers and employers, and why there are fewer
strikes in Switzerland than in other countries, when the textbooks ignore this topic (Mattmüller, 1975:14-15)?

The textbooks that do treat the General Strike agree substantially in their interpretation of this event. According to the authors, it was precipitated by the economic pressures of the war
years, which were most heavily borne by the working classes (Müller, vol. 2:149; Halter:149; Rutsch:241; Chevallaz:420; Pfulg:298;
Weltgeschichte im Bild, 9:94-97).

The French authors observe that the Swiss socialists were
influenced by foreign ideas and inspired by the Russian Revolution (Chevallaz:420; Pfulg:299). "The Swiss socialists during the
war were under the influence of foreign revolutionaries—notably
Russians—who had taken refuge in Switzerland. Among these
was Lenin" (Chevallaz:420).[27] On the other hand, one of the German authors connects the General Strike with the presence of
various undesirable foreign elements:

26. Wir müssen uns bewusst werden, dass der politische Bruder uns näher
steht als der beste Nachbar und Rassenverwandte. Es verlasse sich nur niemand
auf die Freundschaft, die zwischen uns und einem Nachbarvolke in Friedenszeiten
waltet! Vor dem militärischen Kommandoruf und dem patriotischen Klang der
Kriegstrompete verstummen alle andern Töne, auch die Stimme der Freundschaft.
Bei aller Traulichkeit, die uns aus der gemeinsamen Sprache heimatlich anmutet,
dürfen wir dem deutschen Kaiserreich gegenüber keine andere Stellung einneh-
men als gegenüber jedem andern Staat: die Stellung der neutralen Zurückhaltung
. . . Dann stehen wir auf dem richtigen neutralen, dem Schweizer Standpunkt.

27. Les socialistes suisses avaient, durant la guerre, subi l'influence de révo-
lutionnaires étrangers réfugiés en Suisse, russes notamment, parmi lesquels
Lénine.

> Foreign elements infiltrated the cities, especially German deserters
> and Communist agents. . . . Political fanatics wanted to institute the
> "Dictatorship of the Proletariat," using the model of Russia. The
> overwhelming majority of the workers wanted a general improve-
> ment of the position of the lower classes. (Halter:149)[28]

In general, one observes a more conservative outlook in the
German- than in the French-language books. Rutsch, for example,
remarks (p. 241) that the speed with which the strikers gave in to
the parliament and the Federal Council shows that Switzerland is
not a country of passionate revolutionaries: "Our political institutions are anchored too strongly in the people, and an attempt is
made by the welfare state to alleviate vast differences and to help
the weak."[29] Halter (p. 152) concludes that the General Strike
posed a serious threat to the peaceful resolution of differences in
Switzerland:

> The General Strike is a dark page in the recent history of Switzerland.
> Switzerland was at the threshold of a civil war. At fault was the
> fanaticism of some leaders of the workers; equally at fault were those
> who had no compassion for the needs of the common man.[30]

An exception to the generally more conservative tone of the
German Swiss textbooks is revealed in the treatment of the causes
and consequences of the General Strike by the authors of the new
Weltgeschichte im Bild series. They present (9:94-98) a detailed
and objective analysis of the events leading up to the Strike of
1918, and are the only textbook writers to mention the name of
Robert Grimm, a leading Socialist who was instrumental in ar-
ranging it. Furthermore, they use the strike to introduce students
to the proportional system and the parties that emerged between
the two wars. (See also Chevallaz:420-421.)

The other textbook authors merely observe that after the end
of the Strike, the most important demands of the workers were

28. [W]ühlten in den Städten fremde Elemente, vor allem deutsche Deserteure
und kommunistische Agenten. . . . Politische Fanatiker wollten nach russischem
Vorbilde die "Diktatur des Proletariats" aufrichten; die überwältigende Mehrheit
des Arbeitervolkes wünschte eine allgemeine Besserstellung der unteren Schicht-
en.
29. Unsere staatlichen Einrichtungen sind zu stark im Volk verankert, und
der Wohlfahrtsstaat versucht, krasse Gegensätze zu mildern und dem Schwachen
zu helfen.
30. Der Landesstreik ist ein dunkles Blatt der neueren Schweizergeschichte:
Die Schweiz stand vor dem Bürgerkrieg. Schuld daran war der Fanatismus ein-
zelner Arbeiterführer; eine gleich schwere Schuld traf auch jene, die für die Nöte
des kleinen Mannes kein Verständnis zeigten.

met: The 48-hour work week was introduced, wages were revised, and proportional representation in the parliament was instituted (Pfulg:299; Müller, vol. 2:149; Rutsch:241-242).

Recurring Themes in Swiss History

In spite of differing interpretations of some events, there exists a loose framework of recurring themes and attitudes which mold the various cultural groups into a common citizenship. The quest for freedom is an important theme which is brought up time and time again in Swiss history textbooks. This is, in fact, the fundamental idea integrating Swiss history from its beginnings in 1291 through the so-called Heroic Age of the fourteenth century. Thus one reads subtitles such as: "The Waldstätten (founders of Switzerland) fear for their freedom," "The Waldstätten found the Confederation and fight for their independence" (Grandjean:7, 8, 29); "The freedom of the Waldstätten is menaced" (Pfulg:77); "The way to freedom," "The fight for freedom in the Appenzell" (Halter:89, 99); "Freedom efforts in the areas surrounding the Confederation" (Müller, vol. 1:105).

William Tell personifies the tradition of intrepid resistance to foreign oppressors. His name is mentioned in this connection in five of the six textbooks which cover this period, although only three, two French and one German, give a detailed account of his life (Grandjean:9-10; Pfulg:80; Müller, vol. 1:92-93). His name is also recalled in other instances. For example, Müller notes (vol. 2:66) that the leader of the Regeneration in the canton of Aargau (a political movement during the early part of the nineteenth century, dedicated to drawing up new constitutions and placing more power in the hands of the citizens) was heralded as a "new Tell" with all the appropriate symbolism.

All the authors agree that the desire for freedom from foreign oppressors inspired the people from the valleys of Uri, Schwyz, and Nidwalden to sign a pact of perpetual mutual alliance on August 1, 1291. This event formally marked the founding of the Swiss Confederation (Grandjean:13; Pfulg:83; Müller, vol. 1: 85, 90; Hafner:74; Halter:92; Weltgeschichte im Bild, 7/1:40).

Now they were Confederates: united not through blood, but through a voluntary oath. Responsible before God, they wanted to assist each other in fighting for and protecting freedom and rights. (Müller, vol. 1:90)[31]

31. Jetzt waren sie Eid-Genossen: Verbunden miteinander nicht durch Bande

Every year, the national holiday on the 1st of August reminds Switzerland of the founders of the Confederation: a group of intrepid men who were able to defend their rights and their liberties. (Pfulg: 83)[32]

The growth of the Confederation to eight cantons through a variety of alliances was inspired by a common enemy, the Habsburgs, as well as a desire for freedom, according to the textbook authors. The fear of absorption and the quest for freedom also prompted Appenzell, Valais, and the Grisons to enter into alliances with the Confederation. Switzerland was apparently a less objectionable alternative to complete independence than incorporation in a Greater Austria, France, or Germany, however great the cultural attraction of these countries may have been.

The battles of the "Heroic Age" at Morgarten, Sempach, and Näfels are given a central place in the Swiss history texts. Inevitably they were directed toward "the independence of the homeland, and the well-being of the families" (Halter:94).

When speaking of newer battles and situations, the German books, and Hafner in particular, delight in reviving the memory of these wars and the heroic spirit of the old Confederates. One learns of the "old heroic spirit" (alten Heldengeist) of the Bernese at Grauholz, and mourns that the "old spirit of community" (alte Geist der Gemeinsamkeit) which led to the alliance of 1291 and to the growth of the Confederation seemed no longer present at the Diet of 1797 (Hafner:160, 161).

These references are less prevalent in the French-language books. Therefore, one might be inclined to expect less enthusiasm for the old wars in these texts. This does not seem to be the case. Grandjean spends an entire chapter (pp. 25-68) on the battles of Sempach and Näfels, followed by a section on "Switzerland as a big military power" ("La Suisse Grande Puissance Militaire"). Pfulg also gives the old battles a central, but less extensive, treatment.

The quest for freedom is also re-echoed in the later history of Switzerland. Freedom was not, however, synonymous with equality of individual rights—not, at least, until the French occupation

---

des Blutes, sondern durch einen freiwilligen Eid. In gewissenhafter Verantwortung vor Gott wollten sie einander beistehen, Freiheit und Recht zu erkämpfen und zu wahren.

32. Chaque année, la fête nationale du 1er août rappelle à la Suisse entière le souvenir des fondateurs de la Confédération: Un groupe d'hommes intrépides qui ont su défendre leurs droits et leurs libertés.

forced on the Swiss the same human rights which had been proclaimed by the French Revolution. This was not, however, true freedom (Rutsch:55; Jaggi:225-226; Halter:73-75; Chevallaz:74).

Chevallaz observes (p. 66) that, although Rousseau celebrated the direct democracies of the old Swiss cantons as a model of government in *The Social Contract*:

> The reality is less idyllic. Certainly from the age of 14 the men can participate in the Landsgemeinde. However, in fact, there are privileged families which pass on among themselves offices and pension money in a hereditary fashion. Furthermore, these free men have subjects: the people of the Urseren valley and of the Leventina are subjects of the Urners. The Schwyzers of the northern districts are subjects of the Schwyzers of the original canton.[33]

Prior to the French Revolution, freedom had a different meaning for the old Confederates. It meant, as Müller observes (vol. 1: 211; see also Halter:120), freedom for each canton or affiliated territory to conduct its own affairs:

> The oath of the first Confederates—"We want to be one single people of brothers"—must not be misunderstood. They had allied themselves for the preservation of freedom. Freedom meant, however, to be able to live according to their own will. Each canton looked after and preserved its own individuality, and tolerated even within its own territory astonishing diversity.[34]

On numerous occasions, this desire to conduct one's own affairs divided the country into many quarreling sections. Thus, one considered oneself first a Vaudois, or Zurcher, or Bernese. How do the textbook authors treat cantonal and national loyalties? Daalder (1974a:113) suggests that an inspection of the course content of Swiss schools would probably reveal an insistence on both national and subnational alliances, typically regarded as fully compatible.

Indeed, this seems to be the case. While most of the books emphasize the history of their own canton, they appear to do this

33. La réalité est moins idyllique. Sans doute, dés l'âge de 14 ans, les hommes participent à la Landsgemeinde; en fait, il y a des familles privilégiées qui s'attribuent héréditairement charges et pensions. De plus, ces hommes libres ont des sujets: les gens de l'Urseren et de la Leventine sont sujets des Uranais; les Schwytzois des districts septentrionaux sont sujets des Schwytzois du canton primitif.

34. Der Schwurspruch der ersten Eidgenossen—"Wir wollen sein ein einzig Volk von Brüdern"—darf also nicht missverstanden werden. Sie hatten sich zur Wahrung der Freiheit verbrüdert; Freiheit aber hiess: nach eigenem Willen leben können. Jeder Ort hegte und pflegte seine Eigenheit und duldete sogar im Innern erstaunliche Verschiedenheiten.

to instill pride and to inform the student about the canton in which he lives rather than to glorify one part of the country at the expense of the others. On the whole, the textbook authors seem to take for granted that one has dual loyalties to the canton and to the Confederation. The purpose of the Constitution of 1848, they indicate, was to provide for the continued existence of the cantons, as well as to insure the existence of a viable nation.

Diversity is treated by most of the authors with the same basic outlook. By and large it is taken for granted as an aspect of Swiss life. None of the textbook authors indicate that homogenization is a desirable or even possible alternative. Halter writes (p. 112) that cantonal and communal autonomy is of utmost importance:

> It is the old Swiss freedom which our ancestors have been fighting for since the thirteenth century. Thanks to it, German Swiss are able to live differently from the French Swiss or the Ticinese, the mountain people differently from the people living in the lowlands, and the city people differently from the country people. It is also largely responsible for the fact that despite the four cultural groups, Switzerland has never had racial or linguistic strife, and despite the two religions, has seldom encountered religious problems.[35]

Two authors, one German and one French (Müller, vol. 2: 294; Pfulg:275), also express this attitude by quoting Gottfried Keller, a famous Swiss author of the nineteenth century: "How intriguing is it that there is not only one kind of Swiss, but that there are Zurchers, and Bernese, Unterwaldners, and Neuchâtelois, Grisoners, and Baselers, and even two types of Baselers; that there is a history of Appenzell and a history of Geneva. Isn't this diversity in unity truly a school of friendship?"

Furthermore, Müller notes that great Swiss in modern times have seen in the diversity of their country a particular task for the Confederation—to show the world that diverse peoples can live together peacefully. This, of course, does not mean that the textbook authors have neglected the many occasions on which Swiss have fought against one another, or that they are unaware of current problems. Still, they indicate that there are strong forces, historical as well as political, that bind the Confederates together:

35. Es ist die alte Schweizerfreiheit, für welche unsere Ahnen seit dem 13. Jahrhundert gekämpft haben. Ihr verdanken wir es, dass die Deutschschweizer anders als die Welschschweizer oder Tessiner, die Bergbewohner anders als die Bewohner des Mittellandes, die Stadtleute anders als die Landleute leben düfen. Sie hat auch viel dazu beigetragen, dass die Schweiz trotz den vier Volksstämmen nie einen Rassen- oder Sprachenstreit, trotz den zwei Konfessionen seither nur selten konfessionelle Streitigkeiten erlebt hat.

Through the ages she (Switzerland) has experienced religious wars, civil discord, and foreign invasion. The Helvetic community contains —why keep it a secret?—elements of miscomprehension and misunderstanding, germs of division. . . . [But] in the end they drew up a balance sheet of all these adventures. In final account they came to the conclusion that individuals and communities have an interest to patiently support their neighbors, to resolve conflict by arbitration, and to live in friendship with the whole world. (Pfulg:322)[36]

Summary

In summary, we have found that both Protestant and Catholic, German and French Swiss textbooks emphasize political values which transcend narrowly defined cultural interpretations of national history. Clearly, the textbook authors are not immune from presenting a consensus version of history or from putting forth an interpretation of events which favors their own cultural, linguistic, or religious group. But in contrast with textbooks in use in other plurilingual countries, such as Canada and South Africa, Swiss textbooks provide a basis for a positive national identity.

All the books emphasize the importance of decentralized federalism, cantonal autonomy, democratic institutions, and a foreign and domestic policy of neutrality. In addition, historical themes such as the tradition of the Rütli, William Tell, and the fight for freedom are used for the purpose of teaching civic attitudes. Through them are inculcated a love of liberty, resistance to tyranny, courage, shrewdness, and self-reliance.

Diversity for the textbook authors of both language groups is taken for granted as a part of Swiss life. Neither German nor French Swiss view the other language group as a single monolithic entity, nor define one culture in opposition to the other. In general, history is unfolded on a national scale, with reference to individual cantons. Religion, on the other hand, is a more salient source of division. There are indications, however, that it occupies a less dominant role in the newer history textbooks.

Because it is the task of official institutions such as the school

36. Au cours des âges, il a éprouvé les guerres religieuses et les discordes civiles et subi l'invasion étrangère. La communauté helvétique renferme en elle— pourquoi le taire?—des motifs d'incompréhension et de mésentente, des germes de division. . . . Puis ils ont dressé le bilan de toutes ces aventures. En fin de compte, ils ont acquis la certitude que les individus et les communautés ont tout intérêt à supporter patiemment leurs voisins, à résoudre les conflits par l'arbitrage et à vivre sur un pied d'amitié avec tout le monde.

to socialize the consensus values of the society, a survey of Swiss textbooks cannot provide a complete picture of diversity and social relations in Switzerland. The outlook expressed in the official school curriculum may or may not be the one internalized by Swiss youth. To further illuminate the relationship between public opinion and core values in the Swiss setting, the next chapter will focus on young people's attitudes toward multiculturalism.

4 | Diversity and Social Relations in Swiss Society:
The Attitudes of Young People Toward Multiculturalism

What attitudes do young people in Switzerland hold toward multiculturalism? Are cultural diversity and subcultural segmentation (i.e., sharp cleavages of a religious, linguistic, and/or regional or class nature) synonymous in Swiss society? To what degree are language and religion important variables in the formation of attitudes? These are essential and largely unexplored areas in the study of intergroup relations in Switzerland. A survey of attitudes of young Swiss will help us to answer these questions, as well as to paint a more dynamic picture of interethnic relations in this small multicultural society. Furthermore, if the various groups hold similar attitudes, it would cast doubt on one of the major tenets held by consociational theorists—that sharp cleavages in the system can only be bridged by the deliberate efforts of the elites.

Research Procedure

Questionnaires were administered in the fall of 1976 to 538 German- and French-speaking secondary students, aged 14 to 16, in the cantons of Zurich, Bern, Aargau, Solothurn, Zug, Vaud, Neuchâtel, Fribourg, and Valais (see Appendix I for the sample design). The questions focused on young people's attitudes toward diversity in Switzerland: the questionnaire was constructed to investigate various dimensions of pluralism, including multiple loyalties toward state, canton, language, and religion; areas of consensus and cleavage in Swiss life; and core values among the various groups.

Approximately half of the questions were adapted from a study done for the Canadian Royal Commission on Bilingualism and Biculturalism by John C. Johnstone (1969). The other half were drafted specifically for this study. The German and French questionnaires are reproduced in Appendix II.

Awareness of Diversity

One important indicator of an awareness of diversity is provided by estimates of the linguistic composition of the Swiss population. Respondents were asked to gauge what percentage of Swiss spoke German, French, and Italian as their mother tongue. Interestingly, both French and German Swiss overestimate the Italian-speaking population. Presumably this is due to the fact that they include resident foreigners (the majority of whom are Italian-speaking) in their estimates. The data were therefore analyzed in two ways, one taking into account the Swiss population, and the other taking into account the total resident population (see Table 7).

According to the 1970 census, 74 percent of the Swiss population spoke German, 20 percent spoke French, and 4 percent spoke Italian. Answers of 70-79 percent German, 15-24 percent French, and 2-6 percent Italian were therefore recorded as accurate. The distribution of the resident population in 1970, by mother tongue, was 65 percent German, 18 percent French, and 11 percent Italian—thus 60-69 percent, 13-22 percent, and 9-13 percent, respectively, were considered correct answers.

The young people in the sample, whether consciously or unconsciously, seem to include the foreign population in their estimates of the three language communities in Switzerland. The accuracy of the answers, particularly for the German and Italian groups, improves considerably when the resident rather than the Swiss population is used as a base. It is not difficult to understand why secondary students aged 14 to 16 are more impressed by the size of the total resident rather than only the native Swiss language communities. This cohort of young people has witnessed a sharp increase in the Italian foreign-worker population in their own lifetime, and is confronted with their presence every day. They hear Italian spoken on public transportation, on construction sites throughout the cities and towns in Switzerland, and in many public places they visit, such as restaurants and resorts.

Perhaps the most striking finding is the marked degree to which German Swiss underestimate their own presence in the population and overestimate the two minority linguistic communities. If we use the resident population as our standard, we find that over half of the German Swiss underestimate their own number in the population (by 10 percent). In contrast, they overestimate the Italian-speaking population by 3 percent and the French Swiss population by an overwhelming 11 percent. An examination of the French Swiss estimates reveals similar results. While they give a fairly accurate estimate of the Italian-speaking group, the French-speaking Swiss also consistently underestimate the German majority (by 9 percent) and greatly overestimate their own presence in the resident population (by 14 percent).

The findings by Johnstone from a Canadian national sample of young people aged 13 to 20 are in stark contrast. Anglophones and Francophones in the 15-to-16-year-old age category showed a marked tendency to overestimate their own numbers. On the other hand, older Francophones were considerably more likely than younger Francophones to overestimate the Anglophones. The percentage jumped between the youngest and oldest groups from 17 percent to 39 percent. Johnstone (1969:43) concludes: "It would appear that during the adolescent years, Francophones not only become aware of the dominance of the English language in Canadian society, but are so impressed by this fact that they see themselves more in the minority than they really are." This trend is not likely to be found in Switzerland.

What emerges from this study, in short, is that although the German Swiss are a statistical majority, they lack the outlook that is usually associated with this position. The ambiguous feelings the German-speaking Swiss hold about their big neighbor to the north weakens their majority outlook further.[1] Certainly they have not a shred of that sentiment derivative from a perception of being part of a pan-Germanic force.

Tables 8 and 9 highlight this finding. Four different questions were used to measure the tie between the German and French Swiss and various countries. First, the young people were asked to select the countries they consider Switzerland's best friends. A majority of both the German- and French-speaking groups include France and Germany in their selection of Switzerland's three closest friends (Table 8, part B). It is noteworthy that over 50 percent of both groups name Germany. However, the French

1. This same ambivalent feeling appeared when French- and German-speaking youth were asked to rate their relationship with their respective cultural kin. While 81 percent of the French Swiss rated their relationship with France as either good or very good, only 32 percent of the German Swiss gave similar answers when asked about their relationship with Germany.

TABLE 7. Young people's awareness of linguistic composition of resident and Swiss population

Percentage of Swiss which respondent thinks speak German (French, Italian) as their mother tongue

	German-speakers (N = 276)		French-speakers (N = 262)	
	Swiss population	Resident population	Swiss population	Resident population
How many speak German?				
Accurate answer[a]	9.4%	35.2%	15.6%	35.5%
High estimate	1.5	9.4	0.4	16.0
Low estimate	86.3	52.5	79.0	43.5
No estimate made	2.9	2.9	5.0	5.0
Total	100.0%	100.0%	100.0%	100.0%
Mean estimate of German-speakers	55.5%		56.2%	
Standard deviation	9.4		11.9	
How many speak French?				
Accurate answer[b]	17.0%	17.0%	11.8%	11.1%
High estimate	77.9	78.2	82.8	83.6
Low estimate	2.2	1.8	0.0	0.0
No estimate made	2.9	2.9	5.3	5.3
Total	100.0%	99.9%	99.9%	100.0%
Mean estimate of French-speakers	28.5%		32.6%	
Standard deviation	7.6		8.7	

How many speak Italian?

Accurate answer[c]	6.9%	34.4%	21.7%	44.3%
High estimate	90.2	55.1	72.9	25.6
Low estimate	0.0	7.6	0.0	24.8
No estimate made	2.9	2.9	5.3	5.3
Total	100.0%	100.0%	99.9%	100.0%
Mean estimate of Italian-speakers	15.2%		11.4%	
Standard deviation	6.5		6.1	

Accurate answers based on 1970 census data were:

[a]German Swiss, Swiss population 70-79 percent, resident population 60-69 percent.
[b]French Swiss, Swiss population 15-24 percent, resident population 13-22 percent.
[c]Italian Swiss, Swiss population 2-6 percent, resident population 9-13 percent.

Swiss mention France relatively more often (by a margin of 24 percent), while the German Swiss favor Austria and Liechtenstein.

This tendency is even more pronounced if we consider only the country named as Switzerland's closest friend (Table 8, part A). France is named by 40 percent of the French Swiss, compared to 16 percent of the German Swiss. Surprisingly, Liechtenstein is more often identified as Switzerland's best friend (24 percent) by the German Swiss than either Germany (16 percent) or Austria (10 percent). Although Liechtenstein is, of course, not a part of Switzerland, in many ways it is closely linked with its Helvetic neighbor. The principality maintains an embassy in Bern, but

TABLE 8. *Countries named as Switzerland's best friends*

	German-speakers (N = 276)	French-speakers (N = 262)
A. Best friend		
France	15.6%	39.7%
Italy	3.6	2.3
Germany	15.6	11.1
Austria	10.5	5.1
Liechtenstein	23.9	8.0
England	2.9	3.8
United States	7.6	14.1
Others	4.0	5.3
No country named	16.3	10.7
Total	100.0%	100.1%
B. Three best friends		
France	55.8%	79.9%
Italy	27.7	29.9
Germany	50.2	53.4
Austria	44.2	24.4
Liechtenstein	34.6	15.4
England	13.0	18.8
United States	25.1	31.6
Holland	6.1	3.4
All other countries named	16.3	25.5
Total	273.0%	282.3%

otherwise confides its whole diplomatic representation to Switzerland. In addition, there is a customs and monetary union by virtue of which Liechtenstein is entirely absorbed within the Swiss customs area, so that Swiss customs officials collect customs at the frontier of Austria, in offices bearing the joint emblems of both countries. By selecting Liechtenstein as Switzerland's best friend, it appears that German Swiss youth are reaffirming their own identity vis-à-vis Germany and a specifically German culture.

The difference in the rates of no response between the French and German-speaking Swiss also attests to the greater ambivalence of German Swiss youth; 16 percent of the German Swiss, as compared with 11 percent of the French Swiss, did not give definitive answers to this question.

A pattern of forces propelling the two major Swiss linguistic communities toward and away from their big cultural neighbors was also revealed when the respondents were asked in closed- and open-ended questions where outside of Switzerland they would most like to live. When the question was limited to a number of European countries, France was chosen considerably more often than the other countries by *both* the French- and German-speaking Swiss youth (Table 9, part A). Once again a higher percentage of French Swiss youths name France, while the German Swiss responses are split among France, Austria, and Holland. In fact, both groups favor the two latter democracies over Germany, Italy, and Spain, indicating a certain similarity of outlook.

When young Swiss are asked to select the country where they would most like to live on a global basis, much the same picture emerges (Table 9, part B). The French Swiss favor France (chosen by 29 percent), followed by the traditional immigrant countries of the United States (14 percent) and Canada (11 percent). The German Swiss are divided between Austria (15 percent) and France (14 percent), followed by the United States (12 percent), as the countries where they would most like to live. All other countries named were selected by less than 10 percent of the two subsamples.

Finally, forces attracting each of the Swiss language communities toward their respective cultural kin can be seen in Table 10. Respondents were asked how similar or dissimilar they thought each of the following groups: Ticinesi and Italians, Ticinesi and French Swiss, Ticinesi and German Swiss, German Swiss and Germans, German Swiss and French Swiss, French Swiss and French, French Swiss and Germans, and German Swiss and French. The

TABLE 9. *Other country named*
where respondent would most like to live

	German-speakers (N = 276)	French-speakers (N = 262)
A. Other European country in which respondent would most like to live		
Germany	10.2%	9.2%
France	30.1	45.8
Italy	3.6	4.2
Austria	23.2	10.7
Holland	18.1	22.5
Spain	7.2	3.0
No response	7.6	4.6
B. Other country in the world in which respondent would most like to live		
Germany	4.3%	5.7%
France	13.8	29.0
Italy	2.9	1.9
Austria	14.5	4.2
Holland	6.9	6.5
England	8.0	9.2
Canada	8.3	10.6
United States	12.3	13.7
Others	24.7	17.7
No response	4.3	1.5

pairs were perceived as more dissimilar than similar by both groups, with the exception of the Ticinesi and Italians and the French Swiss and French. In most cases, Swiss young people from both linguistic groups attach considerable importance to language and cultural factors when evaluating the similarity or distinctiveness of various groups of people. The one notable exception is the similarity between the German Swiss and Germans: the German Swiss see themselves as rather different (-12 percent) from the Germans, while the French Swiss see these two groups as quite similar (+37 percent).

Another interesting finding concerns the degree of distinctiveness which the French- and German-speaking Swiss youth perceive between themselves and others. These two Swiss linguistic

TABLE 10. Perceived similarity between groups[a]

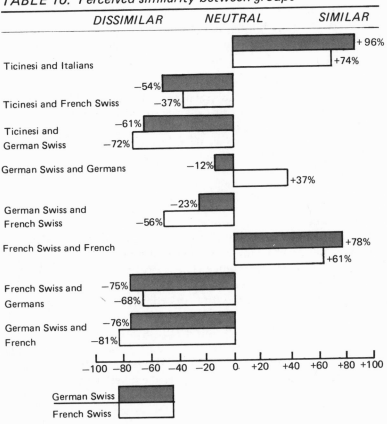

	DISSIMILAR	NEUTRAL	SIMILAR
Ticinesi and Italians			+96% / +74%
Ticinesi and French Swiss	−54% / −37%		
Ticinesi and German Swiss	−61% / −72%		
German Swiss and Germans		−12% / +37%	
German Swiss and French Swiss	−23% / −56%		
French Swiss and French			+78% / +61%
French Swiss and Germans	−75% / −68%		
German Swiss and French	−76% / −81%		

−100 −80 −60 −40 −20 0 +20 +40 +60 +80 +100

German Swiss
French Swiss

[a]The figures represent the percentage discrepancies between those responding that the two groups are very or fairly similar and those responding that they are fairly or very dissimilar. Percentages are computed only for those who gave substantive answers to the questions.

groups see themselves as generally more dissimilar than similar. However, this perception is much stronger among the French Swiss (-56 percent) than among the German Swiss (-23 percent). Nevertheless, we might hypothesize that some sort of "national identity" does intervene in the assessment of the two groups. The French Swiss, while feeling themselves distinct from the German Swiss, sense themselves to be even more dissimilar from the Germans (-56 percent from the German Swiss, as compared to -68 percent from the Germans). For the German Swiss, this correlation is even more pronounced (-23 percent from the French Swiss, as compared with -76 percent from the French).

These findings highlight the observations made by Siegfried (1956:75-76) of the two major linguistic groups. He comments that:

> The sentiments of the Alemanic Swiss toward the Romands, though they may be marked by a secret distrust for the more brilliant defects of the latter, are balanced by a curious partiality for the gifts which they themselves do not possess, and finally by a semi-sentimental attraction to which they surrender themselves almost as to a fantasy. . . . It would be an exaggeration to say that the feeling was reciprocal, but if French-speaking Swiss have no such inclination, at least they have a very strong feeling made up no doubt more of calculation and reason than sentiment.

Together, then, our findings describe a German Swiss majority which is predisposed both to acknowledge and to respect the linguistic minorities. However, these conditions alone are not sufficient for cultural coexistence. The majority as well as the minorities, both linguistic and religious, must hold a positive attachment to the nation and identify with it in order for a stable and harmonious polity to exist.

For the Swiss, the idea of fatherland is not as precise as it is for its major European neighbors, for whom the fatherland is simply France, or Germany, or Italy. As de Rougemont (1965:199) suggests, for the Swiss, fatherland often evokes a smaller entity, connected with the place where one was born, has grown up or has lived. This more local fatherland, however, does not preclude in any way the attachment to other, larger communities, such as Switzerland.

Lüthy (1962:18) goes even further in this comparison, noting that:

> A Breton, Basque, or Alsatian nationalist is very likely to be a bad Frenchman, a Welshman in favor of self-government for Wales will be a doubtful Britisher; in other countries, too, separatist movements endanger national unity. . . . But the believer in self-government for the cantons of Valais or Grisons or Appenzell is a model Swiss patriot, in fact the type of man to whom Switzerland owes her existence. . . . All modern states have come into being through struggling against the regionalism of their component parts; Switzerland, however, was a product of such regionalism and has been sustained in the often serious crises of her history by the local patriotism of her "twenty-two peoples. . . ."[2]

2. The extreme variety of Jurassian nationalism is, however, certainly an exception.

The next section will examine the multiple loyalties of young Swiss adults to the nation, as well as to their canton and their linguistic and religious groups.

Multiple Loyalties

Table 11 shows the strength of various loyalties of Swiss youth in the two major language and religious groups. The responses of all groups—German and French Swiss, as well as their religious segments: German Swiss Catholics and Protestants, and French Swiss Catholics and Protestants—are roughly divided between those believing that cantonal, linguistic, and religious affiliations are important and those who think them unimportant. On the other hand, all the respondents value Swiss citizenship very highly. Our findings thus indicate that national identity for young people in Switzerland today takes precedence over the various other loyalties.

The different groups also make similar appraisals about the various loyalties. This tendency can be seen more clearly when average ratings are ranked. In general, the German Swiss identify slightly more strongly than the French Swiss with the nation, while the Romands express more loyalty toward their religious and linguistic groups and their canton.

Average ratings of affiliation†

	GERMAN SWISS	FRENCH SWISS
National	1.65	1.82
Religious	2.44	2.28
Linguistic	2.46	2.37
Cantonal	2.54	2.49

†Based on scores of 1-4 with low scores indicating higher levels of identification. Excludes those with no opinions. (From Table 11)

Kerr discovered what, at first sight, appears to be a contradictory finding. When asked "Which of these terms best describes the way you usually think of yourself?":

Genevois (for example)
Swiss Romand (for example)
Swiss

40 percent of the French Swiss mentioned the nation, 31 percent their canton, and 29 percent their linguistic group. In contrast, 53 percent of the Alemands identified with the nation, 31 percent with their canton, and 16 percent with their linguistic group. Kerr (1974:21-22) concludes that "the Swiss Alemands have a stronger

TABLE 11. The Strength of various loyalties by language and religious group

	German Swiss (N = 276)			French Swiss (N = 262)		
	Catholic	Protestant	Whole	Catholic	Protestant	Whole
Importance to respondent of being a citizen of his/her canton						
Very important	12.0%	13.7%	12.7%	29.4%	8.7%	22.5%
Fairly important	43.3	23.1	34.1	27.2	24.6	26.7
Not very important	36.0	42.7	39.5	26.1	39.1	29.8
Not at all important	8.7	20.5	13.8	17.2	27.5	21.0
Mean[a]	2.41	2.70	2.54	2.31	2.86	2.49
Standard deviation	.81	.95	.88	1.07	.93	1.06
Importance to respondent of being a German Swiss/French Swiss						
Very important	19.5%	15.4%	17.8%	27.4%	17.4%	23.8%
Fairly important	32.9	30.8	32.0	33.5	30.4	31.8
Not very important	34.2	38.5	36.0	23.5	34.8	27.2
Not at all important	13.4	15.4	14.2	15.6	17.4	17.2
Mean[a]	2.42	2.54	2.46	2.27	2.52	2.37
Standard deviation	.95	.93	.94	1.03	.98	1.03

Importance to respondent of his/her religion

Very important	18.9%	9.4%	15.7%	18.3%	24.6%	21.4%
Fairly important	42.6	34.2	35.3	46.1	36.2	42.0
Not very important	25.7	41.0	32.1	23.3	26.1	23.7
Not at all important	12.8	15.4	16.9	12.2	13.0	13.0
Mean[a]	2.32	2.62	2.44	2.29	2.28	2.28
Standard deviation	.93	.86	.92	.91	.98	.95

Importance to respondent of being a Swiss citizen

Very important	58.0%	49.6%	54.0%	51.1%	42.6%	46.7%
Fairly important	30.0	33.3	31.5	31.1	35.3	33.0
Not very important	8.7	10.3	9.8	8.9	16.2	11.5
Not at all important	3.3	6.8	4.7	8.9	5.9	8.8
Mean[a]	1.57	1.74	1.65	1.76	1.85	1.82
Standard deviation	.79	.90	.84	.95	.90	.95

[a]Based on scores of 1-4, with low scores indicating higher level of identification. Excludes those with no opinions.

sense of specifically Swiss identity than do Swiss Romands, who express a stronger sense of linguistic identification." (See also Sidjanski, 1975.)

These findings do not necessarily imply that French Swiss feel less Swiss than their German-speaking compatriots. In fact, Fischer and Trier (1962:80) conclude in a study of the stereotypes that the two groups hold of each other that "Whereas a Swiss Alemand brings his Swissness into full harmony with his native attachments to the German-speaking part of Switzerland, a Swiss Romand feels, in greater measure, a sense of belonging to the Swiss Romands and, *as such, Swiss.*" In other words, the French Swiss also has an attachment to Switzerland, but his loyalty is less direct than that of the German Swiss.

Still, we have not solved our puzzle. Why do the young Swiss in our sample, be they French- or German-speaking, identify more strongly with the nation than the respondents in Kerr's older national sample?

Table 12 gives a breakdown, by age, of the strength of cantonal, linguistic, and national identification, as well as a pictorial account of the events which have influenced the responses of the different age cohorts. In general, we can observe a movement

TABLE 12. Sense of identity, by language and age cohort

Age	GERMAN SWISS				
Cohort	Cantonal	Linguistic	Swiss	Total	N
20-29	26%	19	55	100	(255)
30-39	29	19	52	100	(236)
40-49	29	15	56	100	(240)
50-59	32	16	52	100	(226)
60-69	39	12	49	100	(211)
70+	42	12	46	100	(137)
Age	FRENCH SWISS				
Cohort	Cantonal	Linguistic	Swiss	Total	N
20-29	24%	21	55	100%	(47)
30-39	35	20	45	100	(54)
40-49	29	38	33	100	(61)
50-59	28	29	43	100	(51)
60-69	23	40	37	100	(52)
70+	43	26	31	100	(54)

AGE COHORTS AND CONTEMPORARY SWISS HISTORY

Year of birth

Year of birth	70-90	60-69	59-59	40-49	30-39	20-29	10-19	
1882								
1887								
1892								
1897								
1902								
1907	▨							Era of radical pre-eminence
1912								
1917		▨						World War I era General Strike
1922								
1927			▨					Initial phases of Depression
1932								
1937				▨				Depression peak; Mobilization
1942								
1947					▨			Postwar recovery and anti-centralist movement
1952								
1957						▨		Prosperity and grand coalition
1962								
1967							▨	Affluence and European Economic Community Association
1972								
1977								

Generation

The formative period from age 15 to 20 of each generation, during which contemporary events have strongest socializing impact, particularly on sense of identity.

Source: Kerr, (1974: 17,23).

away from cantonal identification toward more national identifi-cation, signifying a process of political integration, or nation-building, in Switzerland. However, whereas the sense of attach-ment shifts steadily from the canton to the nation across genera-tions in German Switzerland, one finds abrupt reversals in the progression of national identity among the French Swiss. Kerr (1974:24) believes that these reversals are linked to the formative years of those now aged 40 to 49 and 60 to 69. Among these two generations, whose formative experiences were shaken by the two world wars, one finds the highest levels of linguistic identification.

If Kerr's hypothesis is correct (that minorities react more in-tensely to specific historical experiences), we would expect the youngest generation pictured in his table to have the strongest sense of identification with the Swiss nation. These young Swiss adults, who in 1977 were 10 to 19 years old, have been reared during a time of affluence and tranquility in Switzerland. Our findings support this interpretation and suggest that this age co-hort may have the highest level of national identification to date. Regardless of their linguistic, religious, or cantonal affiliation, they have a strong attachment to their country.

Is this consensus among young Swiss adults also extended to the way they perceive the various levels of government? In order to answer this question, respondents were asked which govern-ment (communal, cantonal, or federal) they felt did the most and the least for the people.

Piaget (1951) has observed that children by the age of 10 or 11 are able to comprehend the notion of "country," that is, to under-stand the territorial relationships between a country as a whole and the various governmental levels which may function within it—communal, cantonal, federal (see Johnstone, 1969:16-17). However, for the Swiss students in this study, the various levels of government and their perceived effectiveness seem to remain part of an adult world with which they can only partially identify. Young people in Switzerland are, of course, aware that Swiss citizens cannot vote or take part in the various levels of govern-ment until they are at least 20 years of age (except in the new canton of Jura, which has set the legal age at 18 years). Also, the functioning of government tends to be less politicized than in many countries. Perhaps these facts help account for the large number from both language groups who responded "I'm not sure." When asked which government did the most for the people, 41 percent of the German-speaking and 26 percent of the French-speaking Swiss did not give a definitive response, while the respective figures are 61 percent and 39 percent for the government thought to be least effective. Apparently the majority language group feels less strongly about the various levels of government.

Because of the large no-response rate, only limited interpretations can be made from these questions. Table 13 does, however, indicate a number of points of similarity and difference in the reactions of the two language groups. Considering the balance between positive and negative assessments in parts A and B of the table, we find that both German- and French-speaking Swiss respond more positively than negatively to the cantonal and communal governments. Among the German Swiss, there is a tendency to regard more highly the governments closest to them. Thus they give the highest net rating to the communal government (+15.8 percent), followed by the cantonal government (+2.6 percent), with the federal government in last position (+1.5 percent).

In contrast with the German Swiss, the French Swiss are more sensitive to the various levels of government. On balance, they believe that the cantonal government is by far the most effective (+16 percent) in doing things for the people. It is followed by the communal government (+8 percent). The federal government, on the other hand, was rated more negatively than positively (-11 percent) by the French-speakers.

Johnstone (1969:20-21) observed a similar phenomenon in his study of young Canadians. The Francophones expressed consistently negative feelings toward the federal government that increased with age, while the attitudes of Anglophones ranged from slightly positive to slightly negative. This disaffection with the federal government is probably a typical minority response of linguistic groups who feel that the cantonal or provincial government is more responsive to their needs.

This difference in attitude toward the federal government between the majority and minority linguistic groups is also linked with the tendency toward more centralization by the federal government. In Switzerland, this development is proceeding against the wishes of the majority of the Swiss people, who persist in regarding cantonal autonomy "as a moral force inherent and complementary to their civic personality." As Siegfried (1956:185) points out, this feeling is particularly strong among the French- and Italian-speaking minorities, who seek to protect themselves against a centralism from which they naturally have more to fear than does the German-speaking majority.

TABLE 13. Orientations to different levels of government

Which government respondent feels does the most for people

	German (N = 276)	French (N = 262)
Federal government	24.9%	27.5%
Cantonal government	13.6	27.9
Communal government	20.8	18.6
I'm not sure	40.8	25.9

Which government respondent feels does the least for people

	German (N = 264)	French (N = 251)
Federal government	9.1%	19.5%
Cantonal government	11.0	12.0
Communal government	19.3	29.9
I'm not sure	60.6	38.6

Direction and strength of orientation[a]

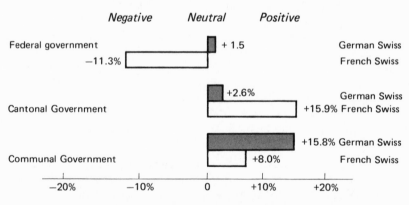

aThe measures represent the percentage discrepancies between positive and negative assessments of the three levels of government. Percentages were computed only for those who gave substantive answers to the questions.

Another indication of a distinctive point of view can be observed in the residential preferences of the French-speaking population. The respondents were asked to indicate which Swiss cantons they would like to live in some day, and also where they would never want to live. Table 14 records the cantons in which 50 percent or more of the two different language groups would prefer to live. Only 6 of the 25 cantons and half-cantons (when the questionnaire was distributed, the Jura was not yet a canton) were named as desirable places to live by the French Swiss. Of these, three are exclusively French-speaking (Vaud, Neuchâtel, and Geneva); one is bilingual: French and German (Valais); one is trilingual: German, Italian, and Romansch (Grisons); and one is Italian-speaking (Ticino). No exclusively German-speaking cantons evoked a majority of positive evaluations.

On the other hand, the German Swiss rated a majority of cantons favorably. Among these are all the cantons named by the French-speaking Swiss. In addition, Lucerne, Bern, Zug, Zurich, Aargau, and Solothurn are favorably evaluated by a majority of German-speaking youth. To some extent, the cantons reflect the composition of the sample. As was to be expected, young people in general gave favorable ratings to their own cantons. Even so, a majority of German Swiss responded positively to cantons outside their own linguistic and cultural influence.

In contrast to Canada, where both Anglophones and Francophones "by no means ignore bilingual and bicultural considerations when thinking about a future place of residence" (Johnstone, 1969:93), this was only true for the French-speaking Swiss. The openness of German Swiss youth toward living in the various cultural and linguistic areas of their country is an important factor in the formula of cultural coexistence in Switzerland.

The next section will deal with attitudes of young Swiss toward multiculturalism and multilingualism. Do young adults share the same beliefs and opinions about their country, and in particular its opportunity structure? How do French- and German-speaking Swiss assess the importance of bilingual skills in their own lives?

Attitudes Toward Multiculturalism and Multilingualism

The way in which different cultural or ethnic groups perceive the opportunity structure of their society has important implications for peaceful intergroup relations. For measuring the impressions of young people regarding the structure of Swiss so-

TABLE 14. Cantons in which respondents would most like to live in the future

| | German Swiss | | | French Swiss | |
Canton	Percentage of positive responses	Number responding	Canton	Percentage of positive responses	Number responding
Lucerne	80.9%	94	Valais	89.4%	141
Valais	78.8	99	Vaud	85.4	89
Bern	78.6	154	Neuchâtel	72.0	117
Grisons	77.2	101	Ticino	70.8	75
Ticino	70.3	145	Grisons	66.3	98
Geneva	70.0	120	Geneva	61.9	147
Neuchâtel	62.2	74			
Zug	59.4	64			
Zurich	57.7	163			
Aargau	51.9	81			
Solothurn	51.3	80			
Fribourg	50.0	96			
Vaud	50.0	74			

ciety, we employed the procedure of Johnstone (1969:8) and asked them to rate ten different factors in helping a young person to get ahead in Swiss life. These evaluations included factors related to both ascribed and achieved status. They therefore allow us to appraise the extent to which members of different groups think the opportunity structure of their society is open or closed.

Table 15 shows the percentages of the two language groups which evaluated each factor as very important. On the average, German and French Swiss differed by 13 percent. This margin is substantially less than that between Johnstone's national sample of Canadian Anglophones and Francophones, which were divided by 20 percent (Johnstone, 1969:8). There was, however, a parallel between the majority and minority views of their respective social structures. On the whole the majority groups in both cultures rated the society as more open than the French-speaking minorities. On the other hand, in contrast to the two Canadian groups, which held widely divergent opinions on the importance of bilingualism (75 percent of the French Canadians, as compared with 39 percent of the English Canadians, rated it as very important in helping a young person get ahead in Canadian life), the French and German Swiss groups were in agreement, both believing that

TABLE 15. *Images of Swiss opportunity structure, by language and religious group*

Percentage who said each factor was very important in helping a young person get ahead in Swiss life

	German (N = 276)			French (N = 262)		
	Catholic	Protestant	Whole	Catholic	Protestant	Whole
Have a good personality	59.5%	68.8%	64.5%	38.7%	25.4%	34.8%
Get good grades in school	64.2	58.1	61.3	45.3	41.8	45.2
Speak both French and German	46.9	45.3	45.8	48.6	32.8	45.5
Get a university education	33.3	40.9	36.5	19.2	42.4	25.1
Be born in Switzerland	19.3	13.2	17.5	20.8	25.8	23.5
Work hard	10.2	26.3	16.7	46.9	34.8	43.7
Know the right people	14.2	7.9	11.1	37.8	37.9	37.5
Come from the right family	8.2	3.4	6.3	11.2	23.4	14.2
Have rich parents	2.7	0.0	1.5	7.6	14.1	8.9
Come from the right religious group	2.1	0.0	1.1	2.4	3.1	3.3

it was a fairly important factor for success in Swiss society (46 percent of both groups thought it was very important to be able to speak both French and German).

Looking at the differences and similarities between German- and French-speaking Swiss, we find that both groups rate the factors related to ascribed status lower than those factors related to achieved status (Table 15). However, the Swiss Romands place slightly more importance on these factors than the German Swiss (social class: "coming from the right family" by 8 percent, economic background by 7 percent, place of birth by 6 percent, and religious background by 2 percent). In addition, French Swiss give a more qualified endorsement to three of the four factors related to achievement (good personality by 30 percent, good grades by 16 percent, and university education by 11 percent). Knowing the right people is also considered much more important by the French-speaking than by the German-speaking Swiss (by 24 percent). Thus, although both groups perceive the Swiss social structure as more open than closed, the French Swiss would appear to do so in much more qualified terms.

Another interesting finding concerns the importance attached by the two groups to work. Contrary to expectation, the French Swiss youth rate working hard much more highly than do their German-speaking compatriots. This probably reflects different cultural interpretations. The average German Swiss takes hard work for granted. Many foreign observers have characterized the German Swiss as conscientious, meticulous workers and respecters of discipline. The temperament of the French Swiss is in marked contrast to that of their German-speaking fellow citizens. It is seen as livelier, more individualistic, and less disciplined (Brooks, 1930:304; Siegfried, 1956:59, 64). Thus it would seem that the Romands are influenced by some of the cultural attributes of their German-speaking neighbors.

Table 15 indicates that the primary variations in assessments occur among the Romands. One must exercise caution in interpretation of the results, due to the composition of the sample. For the most part, the Romand Catholics are from the bilingual, conservative cantons of Fribourg and Valais, while the Romand Protestants are from the more liberal and industrial cantons of Vaud and Neuchâtel. Thus regional considerations also play a part. In general, the French-speaking Protestants appear more cynical about the Swiss opportunity structure than the French-speaking Catholics. They rate two of the ascribed factors higher (economic background by 7 percent, and social class by 12 percent) and two of the achieved factors lower (have a good personality by 13 percent, and hard work by 12 percent). Furthermore, fewer French-speaking Protestants than Romand Catholics (who have considerably more contact with their fellow German-speaking citizens) believe it is important to speak German as well as French. On the other hand, consistent with the so-called "Protestant ethic," the French-speaking Protestants think it considerably more important to obtain a university education.

This tendency is reversed in the German-speaking sample. The German-speaking Catholics perceive the Swiss social structure as slightly less open (placing more importance on knowing the right people, by 6 percent, and social class, by 5 percent; and less value on having a good personality, by 10 percent, working hard, by 16 percent, and getting a university education, by 7 percent), than the German Swiss Protestants. Thus we see that there are intra-linguistic variations between French-speaking Catholics and Protestants, and German-speaking Catholics and Protestants, as well as inter-linguistic differences between French- and German-speakers, as to how the Swiss opportunity structure is perceived. These tendencies help to alleviate potential sources of cleavage within the system.

The reactions of the two language communities toward learning a second national language provide an important indicator of their attitudes toward multilingualism. Lambert has designated two major orientations for the learning of a new language (see Johnstone, 1969:84). A person who primarily wants to broaden his or her cultural horizons—to talk to members of the other language group, or to learn more about their culture—is said to have an "integrative" orientation. When the new language is seen primarily as a steppingstone to some other goal, such as obtaining a job, it is considered an "instrumental" orientation. Several of the situations included in Table 16 reflect either an integrative or an instrumental orientation. Learning the second language to get better grades, find a job, or advance in a career all represent instrumental functions, while learning the second language to talk with friends, to make new friends, to date, or in order to read, or watch television or a movie, are integrative functions. This distinction should help us in discussing the orientation French- and German-speaking Swiss assign to learning German or French.

Table 16 shows the rates at which members of the two groups thought bilingualism would be helpful in various situations. The responses are ranked according to the extent of variation between the two groups. The French- and German-speaking Swiss give

TABLE 16. Perceived functions of bilingual facility

Percentage who said a good knowledge of French/German would be helpful in these ways

	German (N = 276)	French (N = 262)	Difference
In traveling to different parts of Switzerland	93.0%	73.7%	+19.3%
In reading, or watching television or a movie	78.7	64.0	+14.7
In getting better grades in school	88.0	83.7	+ 4.3
In talking with friends	85.4	83.7	+ 1.7
In going out on dates	70.4	68.8	+ 1.6
In finding a job	89.3	93.0	− 3.7
In making new friends	79.7	80.9	− 1.2
In getting ahead in the line of work respondent hopes to enter	84.0	84.5	− 0.5

almost identical ratings on six questions. Only on two items—in traveling to different parts of Switzerland, and in reading or watching TV or a movie—did the French Swiss attach considerably less importance to learning German than the German Swiss did to learning French. These results are consistent with our previous findings. In general, the French minority tends to limit their geographical and cultural interactions to their own territorial and linguistic sphere.

Thus, although there is substantial agreement between the two language groups, it is not surprising that the French-speakers exhibit a more instrumental orientation than the German-speakers to learning a second national language. The French Swiss youth rate finding employment highest, and career advancement second, while the German Swiss most frequently think of French as useful for traveling and finding a job. Both groups rated the functions of dating and cultural enrichment (reading, or watching TV or a movie) lowest.

All in all, whether young French Swiss actually use German to any great extent in their adult life (and there are many indications that they do so far less than German Swiss utilize French), it is important that both language groups believe they will gain similar kinds of benefits from being bilingual.

There are some indications that the importance of both French and German as second languages for Swiss young people is eroding. When asked "What is the most important foreign language for you in the future?" the majority of both linguistic groups named English as their first choice (see Table 17). So far, Swiss educators have had the good sense to require a second national language as a compulsory subject in secondary school. It is unlikely that this position will change in the near future, although on occasion business interests and young students voice the opinion that English is more relevant than French or German. Nevertheless, by placing more importance on a non-official second language, the two linguistic groups run the risk of slowly losing touch with one another.

Returning to Table 17, we find that German was mentioned by a majority of French Swiss and French by a majority of German Swiss as their second language choice. One somewhat striking observation is that twice as many French-speakers in the high-contact areas of Biel and Fribourg as in the other areas named German as the most important foreign language for their future, while the figures remained essentially unchanged for the German Swiss between high- (Biel and Fribourg) and low-contact areas (36 percent compared to 31 percent). Italian, which occupies a weak position in the Confederation as a whole, was mentioned by a small minority of Swiss. However, among this number it is singled out more often by German- than French-speakers.

TABLE 17. Most important foreign languages

Which foreign languages respondent thinks will be most important for him or her in the future

	Most important foreign language	
	German-speakers (N = 276)	French-speakers (N = 262)
French/German	32.3	31.7
Italian	4.9	0.4
English	60.9	67.5
Other languages	1.9	0.4
	Second most important foreign language	
	German-speakers (N = 276)	French-speakers (N = 262)
French/German	54.6	53.5
Italian	11.2	5.0
English	28.8	32.4
Other languages	5.4	9.1

Areas of Consensus and Cleavage in Swiss Life

We measured impressions about national unity by asking young people the extent to which they thought different groups in Switzerland would agree on questions regarding Switzerland's future. These assessments were first made for Swiss as a whole, and then separately for five pairs of groups—Roman Catholics and Protestants, French- and German-speaking Swiss, Swiss and foreign workers, people from rich and poor families, and people from urban and rural areas. The percentage distribution and the mean level of consensus were calculated for all six questions (Table 18). The mean scores were figured by assigning values of between 1 to 5 to the different responses, with low scores indicating higher levels of agreement. Mean scores lower than 3 thus represent a tendency toward consensus, while scores higher than 3 indicate a trend toward dissent.

Both groups felt that Swiss in general would agree more often than disagree. Part A of the table shows that ratings of agreement outnumbered those of disagreement by 26 percent to 17 percent among the German Swiss and 28 percent to 22 percent among the French Swiss.

On the other hand, when asked about the polarities noted above, both groups saw more dissent than consensus among a

TABLE 18. *Areas of perceived consensus and cleavage in Swiss Society*

	German (N = 276)	French (N = 261)
A. Swiss in general Supposing that votes were taken on a lot of questions about the future of Switzerland, does respondent think that the Swiss would agree on most things about Switzerland's future, or that they'd tend to disagree?		
They'd agree on practically everything	1.1%	1.9%
They'd agree on most things	24.6	26.1
They'd agree on half and disagree on half	43.1	34.2
They'd disagree on most things	17.0	19.5
They'd disagree on practically everything	0.4	2.7
I don't know	13.8	15.6
Mean[a]	2.91	2.93
Standard deviation	.73	.87

B. *Religion*
How about Roman Catholics and Protestants—would they agree or disagree on Switzerland's future?

They'd agree on practically everything	7.6%	7.0%
They'd agree on most things	39.1	26.7
They'd agree on half and disagree on half	28.3	27.9
They'd disagree on most things	10.1	18.2
They'd disagree on practically everything	1.8	2.7
I don't know	13.0	17.4
Mean[a]	2.54	2.78
Standard deviation	.89	.99

C. *Ethnicity*
How about French-speaking Swiss and German-speaking Swiss—would they agree or disagree on Switzerland's future?

They'd agree on practically everything	5.8%	2.3%
They'd agree on most things	33.8	23.6
They'd agree on half and disagree on half	35.3	30.9
They'd disagree on most things	12.4	23.9
They'd disagree on practically everything	1.8	7.7
I don't know	10.9	11.6
Mean[a]	2.67	3.13
Standard deviation	.87	.99

D. *Foreign Workers*
How about Swiss and foreign workers—would they agree or disagree on Switzerland's future?

They'd agree on practically everything	0.4%	1.2%
They'd agree on most things	8.0	8.8
They'd agree on half and disagree on half	20.7	22.7
They'd disagree on most things	41.5	36.5
They'd disagree on practically everything	14.5	18.1
I don't know	14.9	12.7
Mean[a]	3.73	3.70
Standard deviation	.87	.95

TABLE 18 cont.

E. *Social Class*
How about people from rich families and people from poor families—
would they agree or disagree on Switzerland's future?

They'd agree on practically everything	0.4%	0.8%
They'd agree on most things	12.1	5.8
They'd agree on half and disagree on half	28.2	15.9
They'd disagree on most things	34.1	38.8
They'd disagree on practically everything	18.7	31.8
I don't know	6.6	7.0
Mean[a]	3.62	4.01
Standard deviation	.96	.91

F. *Place of Residence*
What about people from the big cities and people from the rural
areas—would they agree or disagree on Switzerland's future?

They'd agree on practically everything	1.1%	1.5%
They'd agree on most things	14.5	13.5
They'd agree on half and disagree on half	35.6	33.5
They'd disagree on most things	32.4	32.7
They'd disagree on practically everything	8.0	10.0
I don't know	8.4	8.8
Mean[a]	3.34	3.38
Standard deviation	.89	.92

[a]Based on scores 1-5, with low scores indicating higher levels of
perceived agreement. Excludes those with no opinions.

majority of categories within the population (the French four, and
Germans three, out of the five groups), with levels of agreement
rated slightly higher on all group comparisons by the German
than the French Swiss. Both groups believed that foreign workers
and Swiss citizens, and Swiss from rich and poor families, and
from urban and rural locations, would disagree more often than
agree about Switzerland's future. In addition, the French-speakers
rated relations between German and French Swiss slightly below
the threshold of consensus.

The two groups make similar appraisals on the areas of high
and low consensus in Swiss life. This tendency can be more clearly

noted when the average ratings are ranked. Except for inversions of the fourth and fifth positions, these rankings are identical.

Average ratings of consensus and cleavage
in Swiss society†

GERMAN SWISS		FRENCH SWISS	
Religion	2.54	Religion	2.78
Ethnicity	2.67	Ethnicity	3.13
Urban-Rural	3.34	Urban-Rural	3.38
Social Class	3.62	Foreign Workers	3.70
Foreign Workers	3.73	Social Class	4.01
National	2.91	National	2.93

†Based on scores of 1-5, with low scores indicating higher levels of consensus. Excludes those with no opinions. (From Table 18)

We can conclude from these data that differences between economic classes, and between foreign workers and Swiss citizens, pose the strongest threat to Swiss unity. Urban-rural differences, which to some extent coincide with social class, were viewed as the next most threatening problem. Both language groups agree that consensus would be highest between Swiss Catholics and Protestants, and second highest among French- and German-speaking Swiss. However, the French Swiss are less optimistic on this score.[3]

The average rankings for German Swiss Catholics and Protestants and French Swiss Catholics and Protestants were the same as those illustrated above, but a few significant differences did appear. Among the German groups, the Catholics perceive more dissent among the social classes than do the Protestants (3.70 as compared to 3.53). The opposite was true among the French groups, where the Protestants see more dissent both between economic classes (4.18 as compared with 3.95) and between foreign workers and Swiss citizens (3.83 as compared to 3.64). Again, it would seem that these differences help to offset one another.

3. When asked how they would rate the relations between the two language groups, a similar result was obtained: 53 percent of the German Swiss answered "very good," as compared with 44 percent of the French Swiss. Contact was an important variable among the French-speakers, but not among the German Swiss: 50 percent of the French-speakers from Fribourg and Biel believed the relations were good or very good, as compared to 39 percent of those in other areas. In a smaller and younger sample of Genevans and Lucerners, Melich (1978:132) found that 54 percent of the Genevans and 53 percent of the Lucerners said that the German Swiss and French Swiss were friends (the negative responses were 41 and 42 percent, respectively, with 5 percent of both groups not responding).

Core Values and National Consensus

The final section will once again take up the question of whether young people from different cultural and linguistic backgrounds share similar conceptions and beliefs about their country. Is there a common socio-political culture in Switzerland to which the different groups can relate?

Several authors have suggested that Switzerland, unlike many multicultural societies, has a set of common values underlying its diverse linguistic and religious groups (see Naroll, 1964: 4-9). Heiman (1966:338), in comparing the Swiss with the Canadian situation, notes:

> Whether he is of French Swiss, German Swiss, or Italian Swiss background, the citizen of that country subscribes to one common political tradition. Such is not the case in Canada.

While there is an extensive literature to support this statement in Canada—in particular, studies dealing with the attitudes of young people (Johnstone, 1969; Lamy, 1975; Richert, 1974)—very few investigators have attempted to identify whether there is, indeed, a common tradition underlying Swiss ethnic pluralism. This section examines the people, events, and values Swiss young people most often associate with their nation.

One dimension of cultural identification was investigated by asking Swiss young people to write down the names of important persons in their country's history. In a similar study, Richert (1974) found that Canadian Anglophones and Francophones identified primarily with symbols of their own cultural group. In addition, the students identified with different eras of Canadian history—the French Canadians with the period prior to 1760 (the date of the fall of New France), and the English Canadians with a slight preference for the post-1760 era. Do French- and German-speaking Swiss also reveal this duality? What historical figures do young people in Switzerland identify with?

Table 19 lists the historical persons most often mentioned by these young Swiss. The percentages recorded exclude those who did not respond to this question. It appears that the French Swiss had more difficulty identifying Swiss personalities than did their German-speaking compatriots. The no-response rate for the French Swiss is three times greater (34 percent as compared to 11 percent) than for the German Swiss. However, if we focus our investigation on those who did reply to this question, we find that a similar pattern emerges.

TABLE 19. Most-cited historical figures

German Swiss (N = 276)		French Swiss (N = 262)	
William Tell	36.3%	William Tell	32.2%
Henri Dunant	14.7	Henri Guisan	13.2
Arnold Winkelried	11.4	Niklaus von Flüe	11.5
Henri Guisan	11.4	Arnold Winkelried	6.9
Johann Heinrich Pestalozzi	5.7	Founders of Switzerland	4.0
Niklaus von Flüe	5.3	Johann Heinrich Pestalozzi	4.0
Ulrich Zwingli	4.5	Jean-Jacques Rousseau	3.4
Adrian von Bubenberg	1.2	Henri Dufour	2.9
Henri Dufour	1.2	César Frédéric La Harpe	2.3
		Jean Calvin	1.7
		Henri Dunant	1.7
		Major Davel	1.7
Total	91.7%		83.5%

In contrast with the Canadian results, the two Swiss groups are in substantial agreement. German Swiss heroes are referred to by 70 percent of the German Swiss and 73 percent of the French Swiss, while 30 percent of the German-speaking and 27 percent of the French-speaking Swiss named Romand heroes. Except for Nello Celio (a past Federal Councillor), who was only mentioned a couple of times, figures from the small Italian group were ostensibly missing. Apart from this omission, the percentages of heroes from the two cultural groups are in almost exact proportion to the population. The prevalence of German Swiss heroes is also related to the history of the Confederation. The French Swiss cantons, with the exception of Fribourg (which was incorporated in 1481), did not join Switzerland until the beginning of the nineteenth century.

Over five decades ago, Brooks (1930:5) observed that the Swiss have little admiration for statesmen; their heroes are all dead heroes.[4] This still seems to be the case. Not only are they dead heroes, but they appear to be mythological ones as well. Whether William Tell is a real or only a legendary character is in fact a

4. A few present and past Federal Councillors were named: Pierre Graber, Rudolf Gnägi, Kurt Furgler, Georges-André Chevallaz, Ernst Brugger, Nello Celio, and Rudolf Minger. However, even when they are coded together they were mentioned by only 4 percent of the German- and French-speaking Swiss youth.

subject of current debate.[5] Nevertheless, he stands out as the most-often-mentioned hero. Most Swiss were in agreement with the reason given by a German Swiss student from Solothurn who wrote, "He helped to free Switzerland from her oppressors. He is our national hero." As such, he transcends cultural and religious boundaries.

The legend and the symbol of William Tell are inadvertently reinforced in the minds of Swiss young people in a number of ways. In many cities, large and small, a special school matinée of Schiller's play is a time-honored way of introducing pupils to the study of Swiss history. In addition, his image appears on the five-franc piece (the so-called *Fünfliber*).

Over 50 different historical figures were referred to, but only 9, by the German Swiss group, and 12, by the French group, were mentioned by more than 1 percent of the respondents as their first choice. An examination of the 9 most-named figures reveals that 6, or two-thirds of the symbols, appeared on both lists: William Tell, Arnold Winkelried (the legendary hero of the battle of Sempach), Henri Guisan (the commander of the Swiss army during World War II), Johann Heinrich Pestalozzi (the famous Swiss educator who advocated education for the masses), Niklaus von Flüe (a Swiss monk who is credited with saving Switzerland from internal war), and Henri Dufour (the general of the federal forces during the Sonderbund war). All of these figures played a conciliatory role in Swiss history. Interestingly, not one Swiss youth mentioned Ulrich Wille, the Swiss general during World War I, or Johann Ulrich von Salis-Soglio, the general of the Sonderbund troops.

Henri Dunant (the founder of the Red Cross) and the three founders of Switzerland also provide interesting examples of heroic figures which transcend cultural boundaries. Henri Dunant, a Genevan, is named almost exclusively by German Swiss youth, while the three founders of Switzerland, who were obviously German Swiss, are mentioned more often by French Swiss.

Although a portrait of cultural unity emerges with respect to the heroes named, there are also discrepancies in some of the details painted. Adrian von Bubenberg (the Bernese commander at the battle of Murten) was mentioned exclusively by German Swiss, mainly from the canton of Bern, while Major Davel, the

5. Melich (1978) also observed in her sample of young Swiss aged 9-13 that William Tell was the most recognized Swiss figure. For an interesting account of the position and symbol of William Tell in Switzerland, see Otto Marchi, "Wilhelm Tells geschichtliche Sendung" (1975).

leader of a Vaudois revolt against Bernese rule, is named exclusively by French-speaking Vaudois youth. Likewise, Jean-Jacques Rousseau and César Frédéric La Harpe (one of the fathers of the "Helvetic Republic") were named only by French Swiss. Sometimes the patterns are even more complicated. Niklaus von Flüe is referred to by a considerable number of French Swiss Catholics, but is totally ignored by the French Swiss Protestants. On the other hand, he is mentioned by almost equal numbers of German-speaking Catholics and Protestants.[6] Zwingli is mentioned more often by German Protestants than Catholics, but seldom cited by French speakers of either faith. Surprisingly, Calvin received few nominations by any group, which may point to the greater secularization of Protestant Romand youth. The number of respondents from Neuchâtel and Vaud (traditionally French-speaking Protestant cantons) who said they did not belong to any religion was greater than in any of the other cantons.

When the two language groups were asked to name the most important battle in Swiss history, a similar pattern emerged. Both German- and French-speaking Swiss are most impressed by the old battles against foreign enemies (see Table 20). The battles of Morgarten (1315) and Sempach (1386), the Burgundy Wars (which involved the battles at Murten, Grandson, and Nancy in 1476-77), and the battle of Marignano (1515) are named by 94 percent of the German-speaking and 97 percent of the French-speaking Swiss. The battles omitted are as interesting as those included. The religious battles between Swiss cantons are seldom mentioned.

Returning to Table 20, we find that the German Swiss mentioned the oldest battles more often (Morgarten by a margin of 17 percent, and Sempach by 7 percent), while the French Swiss identified more readily with the two later battles (the Burgundy Wars by a margin of 17 percent, and the battle of Marignano by 11 percent). This difference may be related both to the time of association of the French-speaking cantons with the Confederation and the practice of emphasizing historical events closer to home.

In sum, we have seen that the fight for freedom captivates the imagination of all Swiss. It is symbolized in heroes and battles which are overwhelmingly chosen by French and German Swiss of both faiths. Swiss history teachers are sometimes accused of

6. Siegfried (1956:143-144) observes that the canonization of Niklaus von Flüe in 1947 did not take place without causing some emotion in Protestant circles. To turn a national hero into a Catholic hero suggested a breach of an unwritten neutrality. Interestingly, our study shows that the French Protestants have not accepted him as a national hero as has the rest of Switzerland.

TABLE 20. *Most important battle*

	German Swiss	French Swiss
Morgarten (1315)	45.2%	28.5%
Sempach (1386)	10.9	3.4
Burgundy Wars (1476-77)	30.3	46.9
Marignano (1515)	7.2	17.9
Total	93.6%	96.7%

"burying themselves in epochs, safely remote from the hurly-burly of modern politics," or at least of finding it convenient to stop with the Old Confederation (1789) or the Act of Mediation (1815), leaving students ignorant of more modern events (Brooks, 1930:184). Whether this is deliberate or whether, as many students told me, "time simply runs out" before digesting all of Swiss history is difficult to say. Nevertheless, it appears that with few exceptions the *"Freiheitskampf"* or *"la lutte pour l'indépendence"* and the heroes connected with it serve to build the foundation of a Swiss culture.

Upon this common foundation, we have observed that there also seems to exist "a certain Swiss outlook" which unites Helvetic citizens of different linguistic and religious backgrounds. Siegfried (1956:140-141) and McRae (1964:21) suggest that all Swiss, no matter who they are, hold fast to their communal and cantonal autonomy, based on a direct or quasi-direct consultation of the people in matters which concern the administration of their community. In addition, they share characteristic institutions such as the collegial organization of executive power and a nonprofessional citizen army.

Do young Swiss also share this common outlook? What, in their eyes, are the factors which make them proud to be Swiss? What differences exist between the various groups? In order to answer these questions, young people were asked to write in a few sentences why they were proud to be Swiss, as well as what they did not particularly like about Switzerland. Approximately 50 reasons were mentioned in response to both questions. These, and the method of coding these questions, appear in Appendix I.

The reasons why young people say they are proud to be Swiss are classified into 9 categories. The first category covers political responses. Typical answers are that Switzerland is democratic (having the right to vote, and the rights of initiative and referen-

TABLE 21. Reasons given for being proud to be Swiss[a]

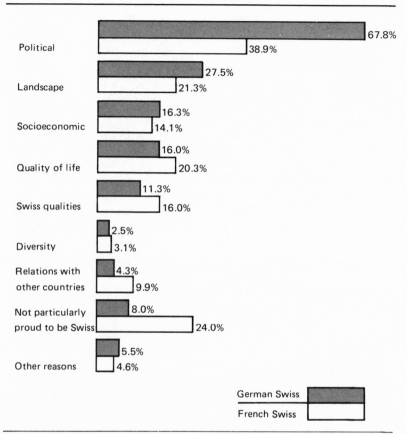

	German Swiss		French Swiss

[a]The percentages refer to those who gave one or more answers in each category among a possible 5 coded responses.

dum), is a neutral country, is not involved in wars and does not attempt to make wars. In addition, many note that one is free in Switzerland (having freedom of speech and the right to travel wherever one wants, as opposed to Eastern European countries). As Table 21 shows, political responses were given considerably more often than any other reasons, which confirms that young people in Switzerland, even before they reach adulthood, seem to have a "certain Swiss outlook." Once said, it should be noted, however, that the two language groups vary considerably in the frequency with which they give this response. The German Swiss give political answers almost twice as often as their French-speaking compatriots.[7] This is not entirely surprising, since most of the political institutions of Switzerland were inherited from German Switzerland.

It appears that what pulls people of heterogeneous origins into a common citizenship in Switzerland—as in the United States[8] —is an abstract concept jointly held of what the state should be. In other words, the state (or Switzerland) stands for something in the eyes of Swiss youth. This is a critical element, particularly in countries divided by language, religion, and/or ethnicity. When a unified political culture is absent, it is difficult for citizens in plural societies to obtain a positive national identity. Unlike Swiss and Americans, Canadians tend to base their national pride on other than political values. Hodgetts (1968) found that most Anglophone twelfth-grade students admired their country mainly for its geographic features—the beauty of the land and its natural resources. French Canadian youth, on the other hand, were primarily proud of their ability to survive as a people. The lack of devotion to a "common outlook" has rendered a Canadian identity difficult.

Returning to Table 21, we observe that there is substantial agreement about 6 of the remaining 8 categories. The second-most-named set of reasons had to do with the landscape of the country. Approximately one-fourth of both linguistic groups said they identified with Switzerland because of its natural beauty. Factors associated with the Swiss quality of life came next (tranquil, clean, orderly) and the characteristics exhibited by the Swiss people (hard-working, self-sufficient, possessing common sense), followed by socioeconomic reasons (such as the small difference between rich and poor, the high standard of living in Switzerland, and the absence of unemployment).

On the other hand, more than twice as many French-speaking

7. On the whole, the Swiss Romands tend to be more critical of the political institutions of Switzerland than their German-speaking fellow citizens. For example, 8 percent of French Swiss as compared to 1 percent of German Swiss recruits in the military thought that the international recognition of Swiss neutrality was enough and that the army was therefore not necessary. Likewise, only 40 percent of the French Swiss thought that Switzerland was still definitely a neutral country, as compared to 51 percent of the German Swiss (*Bericht über die pädogogischen Rekrutenprüfungen im Jahre 1968*, 1969:66, 110). Glass (1975) also found that the French Swiss are more critical of the state than the German Swiss. French-speakers, however, are less willing than German-speakers to endorse political violence.

8. Almond and Verba (1963) found that the majority (85 percent) of American adults associated their national identity with a civil value—attachment to democratic political institutions.

(10 percent) as German-speaking youth (4 percent) are impressed with Switzerland's relations with other countries. Among the factors noted are: that Switzerland plays a fairly large role (in comparison to its size) in world affairs, it is the seat of many world organizations, Switzerland is a well-respected country, etc. The close proximity of French Switzerland to Geneva is one probable reason that French Swiss are more aware of relations with other countries.

Two interesting observations stand out with respect to majority-minority relations in Switzerland. First, it is striking how few young Swiss mention diversity as a source of pride in their country. It seems that most Swiss have come to take the heterogeneity of their country for granted, regarding the multiplicity of languages or religions neither as a particular advantage nor disadvantage, but rather as a marriage of convenience. Nevertheless, the German-speaking partner seems to feel more at home in Switzerland. Three times more French Swiss (24 percent) than German Swiss (8 percent) reply that they are not particularly proud to be Swiss, or that they could just as easily be citizens of other countries. In part this response may reflect the more carefree and less rigid temperament of the French Swiss.

Turning now to the reasons young people give as to why they are not particularly proud to be Swiss, we find that both groups also give similar responses (Table 22). Only three factors warrant further comment. First, it is noteworthy that both groups rated the restrictiveness and the mentality (which are considered together by many of the respondents, and therefore coded in one category) of the Swiss as the feature they dislike most. It should be noted, however, that the French Swiss give this response considerably more often than the German Swiss (23 percent as compared to 14 percent). The French-speakers are more critical of the Swiss mentality because they believe it to be different from their own. Fischer and Trier (1962:70) found that there is a close affinity between the stereotypes that the German Swiss hold of themselves and of Swiss in general. On the other hand, there is relatively little convergence between the stereotypes the French Swiss paint of themselves and of all Swiss—the latter instead resembles their portrait of the German Swiss.

This same sensitivity is apparent when we look at the attitudes of the two groups toward diversity. Twice as many French- (10 percent) as German-speaking Swiss (5 percent) express a dislike or at least an ambiguous feeling toward diversity. And, relieved from a similar concern with their position in the Confed-

TABLE 22. Reasons given for not being proud to be Swiss[a]

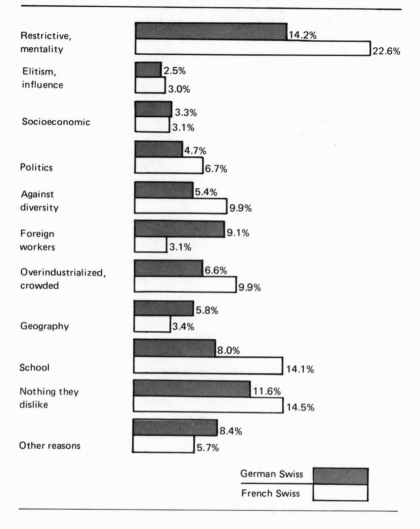

	German Swiss	French Swiss
Restrictive, mentality	14.2%	22.6%
Elitism, influence	2.5%	3.0%
Socioeconomic	3.3%	3.1%
Politics	4.7%	6.7%
Against diversity	5.4%	9.9%
Foreign workers	9.1%	3.1%
Overindustrialized, crowded	6.6%	9.9%
Geography	5.8%	3.4%
School	8.0%	14.1%
Nothing they dislike	11.6%	14.5%
Other reasons	8.4%	5.7%

[a]The percentages refer to those who gave one or more answers in each category among a possible 5 coded responses.

eration, the German Swiss population identifies more readily with other internal problems. The foreign-worker problem was named as a reason why they are not proud to be Swiss by 9 percent of the German Swiss, as compared to 3 percent of the French Swiss. Among the answers given, approximately two-thirds are ashamed of the way the foreign workers are treated, while the other third believe that there is an excessive number of foreigners in Switzerland.

Summary

Several attitudes deeply rooted in the Swiss political culture assist in accommodating the diverse linguistic and cultural interests in Switzerland. We have seen that the Swiss Germans, although a statistical majority, do not possess what may be called a "majoritarian outlook."[9] As a group, German Swiss youth seem willing to acknowledge the diversity of their country. They overestimate the linguistic minorities and underestimate their own number in the population. The opposite is true of the French Swiss, who overestimate themselves and underestimate the German-speaking population. In combination, these trends produce a healthy respect for the linguistic minorities by the majority language group, as well as a more self-confident French-speaking minority.

This tendency is strengthened by a number of factors. From a residential point of view, the German-speaking youth do not confine their positive evaluations to cantons located within their own linguistic and cultural influence. This attitude is not reciprocated by the French Swiss, who feel more secure in cantons where they predominate. On the other hand, the linguistic equilibrium between French and German Switzerland is strengthened by a common understanding between both parties on the importance of bilingualism.

At least two conditions unique to Switzerland also contribute to the cohesion of the society. First, we have observed an unusual case of cross-cutting. Although the two linguistic groups do not project the same picture of the opportunity structure in Switzerland, the various images are softened by counteracting religious tendencies within the two linguistic communities. In general, the German Protestants and French Catholics see the Swiss social structure as more open, while the opposite view is more prevalent among the German Catholics and French Protestants. The differential centrifugal tendencies between the two linguistic groups toward their respective cultural kin provides a second factor of

9. Glass (1975) also concludes in an extensive reexamination of two national opinion surveys that, in contrast to many other segmented polities, no national cultural subgroup manifests any particular sense of disadvantage. The only exception is the French-speaking Jurassian group in the canton of Bern.

equilibrium between French and German Swiss. For historical reasons, the cultural attraction of German Switzerland toward Germany is weaker than the comparable force propelling French Switzerland toward France.[10] As a consequence, the German Swiss attempt to distinguish themselves from their formidable neighbor to the north, a situation which in fact creates a stronger tie with their French-speaking fellow citizens.

While German Swiss do not have the majoritarian outlook that their numbers would seem to predict, the opposite is not entirely true of the French linguistic minority. This sensitivity can be detected in a variety of responses. Three times as many French Swiss as German Swiss answer that they are not particularly proud to be Swiss. In addition, they are more reserved in their evaluation of the opportunity structure and the federal government in Switzerland. An appraisal of the cleavage structure shows that the Romands perceive more dissent between French- and German-speaking Swiss than do their Alemanic compatriots. On the other hand, other cleavages (those between rural and urban, foreign workers and Swiss citizens, and rich and poor) stand out in their eyes as even more salient sources of division within Switzerland.

In Canada, many of the same minority responses are observable among the French Canadians. However, in contrast with Switzerland, there are few factors to mitigate these feelings. Adolescent Francophones underestimate their numbers in the Canadian population, while many Anglophones in the 15- to 16-year-old category believe they are more numerous than they actually are. Furthermore, the commitment to bilingualism seems to be much more apparent among Canadian Francophones. When questioned about the value of being able to speak both French and English in helping a young person to get ahead in Canadian life, 34 percent more 15- and 16-year-old French than English Canadians evaluated it as being very important. It is hardly surprising, then, that both groups perceive the cleavage between French and English as the most threatening to national unity.

In Canada, one is faced with a situation where majority and

10. German Switzerland expressed great admiration for the Germany of 1914. Even the German defeat in 1918 was not altogether sufficient to open the eyes of the German Swiss. However, Hitler's Germany was too much for these democrats and produced an almost instinctive and violent reaction. There was even a tendency to speak Swiss German on occasions when it had not formerly been used. More than a quarter of a century after World War II, German-speaking Swiss youth still feel ambivalent toward their big neighbor to the north.

minority meet head on. While the response of the French Canadian linguistic minority differs in degree but not in kind from the French-speakers in Switzerland, a comparable analogy cannot be made for the English-speaking Canadian majority. Unlike the German Swiss, the Anglo Canadians hold a majoritarian outlook vis-à-vis the Francophone minority. The differential response between the majority language groups in Switzerland and in Canada provides one of the most striking contrasts between the two countries. The gloomy assessment put forward by M.G. Smith that "Cultural diversity or pluralism automatically imposes the structural necessity for domination by one of the cultural sections" (Lijphart, 1977a:18) need not be the case.

The results of this study also suggest several interesting reflections on, and perhaps limitations of, the consociational model, at least as applied to Switzerland in the 1970s. One major approach to consociationalism is that the social cleavage or cleavages in the society must be sufficiently intense and durable to maintain organized segmentation.[11] What happens when these conditions are no longer met?

Although the religious-ideological cleavage, which has historically been the most important in Switzerland, became the basis and model for subsequent organization, one wonders if it can continue to serve as a rallying point among a new generation of Swiss citizens. Swiss youth still attach considerable importance to their religion. However, French and German Swiss of both faiths now rate the religious cleavage lowest in importance. This view was also expressed when young Swiss were asked the salience of several factors in helping young people get ahead in Swiss society. Religion was rated by all four groups as the least important factor.

A second approach to consociationalism, associated primarily with the work of Lijphart, singles out the capacity and good will of the elites. However, by emphasizing the conscious and deliberate efforts of autonomous elites, it neglects the role of popular opinion and even suggests that it plays a negligible role in sustaining harmonious interethnic relations. Our study suggests that, rather than working as autonomous elements in the society, the elites have a broad base of support from the citizenry. Moreover, this base is buttressed by a common socio-political foundation, or what might be called a civic culture, that unites Swiss of diverse backgrounds. In short, the predominant pattern today in Swit-

11. See McRae (1974:5-8), "Introduction" to *Consociational Democracy*, and the references quoted therein.

zerland seems to be one of cultural diversity rather than subcultural segmentation.

We shall explore the implications of these findings in more depth in the concluding chapter. First, however, we shall turn our attention to sources of intergroup conflict which challenge the prevailing picture of Swiss harmony.

5 | Contemporary Problems

The picture of Swiss coexistence is blemished by two problematic issues, the political status of the Jura and the fate of the *Gastarbeiter*, or foreign workers. To explore these unsettled questions of intergroup tensions in Switzerland today, it is necessary to take an excursion into both local and national politics. Like most difficulties within the Swiss system, the Jura conflict emerged primarily at the local level over competing goals among groups claiming different ethnic allegiances. As such, it offers a test case in the politics of conflict regulation in the Swiss setting. The foreign worker problem, on the other hand, concerns a voiceless non-national political minority. While it is part of the uneven development and internationalization of the labor force (Castells, 1975), and therefore outside the immediate concern of this work, on a national level it challenges the capacity of Switzerland, with its complex balance of ethnic forces, to fairly treat a new minority.

The Jura Question[1]

The troubles in the Jura are rooted in the confusion left by Napoleon's new order. Before 1789 the Jura districts had belonged to the prince-bishop of Basel, who from the tenth century onward ruled the Jura and other adjacent territories within the framework of the Holy Roman Empire. During the Reformation, Basel as well as the South Jura became Protestant, while the North Jura remained Catholic.

With the French Revolution, the Old Regime was dismantled,

1. This section benefitted greatly from numerous discussions with Kenneth McRae.

125

and for more than two decades the Jura remained under the rule of France. During this time new ideas of democracy were implanted and new institutions were introduced: a centralized administration and the Napoleonic Code. After the fall of Napoleon in 1814, the victorious powers met in Vienna in order to reestablish peace and to regulate European borders. Among other Swiss questions, such as the fate of Vaud and Aargau and the destiny of the Gex territory adjacent to Geneva, the Congress of Vienna was also obliged to deal with the political future of the Jura. After considerable squabbling, the Congress finally awarded the Jura district to Bern as compensation for Bernese territorial losses in Vaud and Aargau. Neither Bern nor the former bishopric was entirely satisfied: acquiring mountainous terrain at the expense of Mittelland left Bern disgruntled, and becoming Bern's unwanted acquisition left most Jurassians nostalgic about the bishopric. Furthermore, McRae (1978) observes that unlike the other plurilingual cantons, which developed linguistic pluralism within organically integrated communities, the new canton of Bern formed by the addition of the Jura territory was a product of European diplomacy.

During the next century and a half, many events served to aggravate the situation between the Jura and the old canton. Table 23 indicates the main periods of Jura separatism and its most salient features through 1979. A serious source of friction in the century following the Act of Union in 1815 centered around religion. The most important violation took place in 1836 when the new liberal government in Bern, inspired by the Articles of Baden, attempted to nationalize the Catholic Church. These Articles included provisions which subjected the Catholic clergy to popular vote, and required a loyalty oath by the clergy to the canton. Troubles broke out in the North Jura, and Bern backed down only after France threatened to intervene in favor of the Jurassians.

In the 1860s and 1870s, even more serious and prolonged troubles arose with the *Kulturkampf*. The dispute between liberal cantonal authorities and the Catholic Church culminated with Pope Pius IX's declaration of papal infallibility. The Swiss cantonal governments feared the potential dependence of their clergy on Rome. In 1873, Bern demanded that the Catholic clergy break off religious communication with Lachat, the bishop of the diocese of Basel within whose territory Bern fell. The cantonal order was ignored by 92 priests from the Jura. In rebuke, the cantonal government sentenced them to fines and imprisonment (Bonjour,

1952:297). Although pacification came less than five years later, these events left a heritage of bitter memories in the Catholic Bernese Jura. The French-speaking communes that were affected by the repercussions of the *Kulturkampf* of the 1870s were the same ones, with one or two exceptions, which later were to support the 1974 plebiscite for a separate canton.[2]

Linguistic awareness in the Jura was limited except for the sensitive period surrounding World War I, when the district became caught up in the tide of pan-Germanism originating outside Switzerland. It gained sudden importance three decades later when it was sparked by a display of cantonal insensitivity. In 1947, the Jurassian Georges Moeckli was unanimously nominated by the Bernese government to the cantonal post of Director of Public Works. His appointment was opposed by Hans Tschumi, a deputy from Interlaken, on the grounds that a post of that importance should be headed by a man whose mother tongue was German. Tschumi's motion to reject the nomination was carried. This action incited indignation from the French-speaking Jura population. However, a motion to reconsider Moeckli's appointment was lost by two votes (Harder, 1978).

The language question temporarily united both Protestant and Catholic, north and south, in the *Comité de Moutier*. The committee's efforts eventually led to amendments to the cantonal constitution in 1950, which recognized the identity of a *"peuple jurassien"* and granted equal status to French and German as cantonal languages. In addition, Jurassians were guaranteed at least two of the nine seats on the cantonal executive body.

Some factions, especially in the North Jura, remained unsatisfied with this solution. Thus during the 1950s a new movement, the *Rassemblement jurassien*, gained ground in the north and began a popular initiative for a separate canton. In 1959 this referendum was defeated, overwhelmingly in the old canton and even, narrowly, in the Jura itself. Only the three northern districts of Delémont, Porrentruy, and Franches-Montagnes approved it by strong majorities.

Realizing that they were a minority of the total population of the canton, and even of the Jura as a whole, the Rassemblement jurassien deliberately chose to escalate the conflict to draw attention to its plight. In 1962 a small group of Jurassians, probably not numbering more than 20, founded the *Front de Libération Jurassien* (FLJ), and between 1962 and 1964 set fire to two military instal-

2. For an account of the history of the Jura see Bessire (1935), Gasser (1965), Henecka (1972), Phillippe (1979), and Prongue (1973).

TABLE 23. Main periods of Jura separatism and its most salient features

Parameters of the conflict	1826-1831	1834-1836	1838-1839	1867-1878	1913-1915	1947-1979
General situation	Penetration of liberal ideas	Religious conflicts in Switzerland 'Baden Article'		Kulturkampf	Pan-Germanic tendencies Split between Swiss French and Swiss Germans during World War I	Emergence of a post-industrial society
Explicit causes	Authoritarian control by Bern Jura's cultural identity	Same as 1826-31, plus the anticlericalism of the Bern government	Same as 1826-31 and 1834-36	Discrimination against Jura Catholics	Tendency to Germanize the Jura	The Moeckli affair: the Bern government refused the nomination of a person from the Jura to the post of State Advisor for the Department of Public Works because French was his mother tongue

Aim of the movement	Creation of a canton or an autonomous region	Creation of a canton Attachment to France	Defend the traditions of the Jura Creation of a canton of Jura	Creation of a canton of Jura	Creation of a canton of Jura or of two half-cantons, north and south	Creation of a canton of Jura or of two half-cantons or of a North Jura canton or of an autonomous Jura within the canton of Bern A new canton of Jura came into existence on January 1, 1979
Separatist movement leaders	Intellectuals from the Collège de Porrentruy 'Cercle Stockmar' Liberal groups	Catholic intellectuals from the Collège de Porrentruy Catholic Conservative party	Various Jura parties	Catholic Conservative party	Catholic Conservative party	The 'Rassemblement jurassien' The Christian Social party The young from various movements

TABLE 23 cont.

Opponents	Bern government	Liberal party and Bern government	Bern government	Liberal radical party Bern government	Bern government	Bern government Liberal radical party The 'paysans artisans et bourgeois' party The 'Union des patriotes jurassiens'
Most adamantly separatist regions	Porrentruy	North Jura	Porrentruy	North Jura	North Jura	North Jura

Source: Adapted from Bassand (1975:142-143).

lations and bombed a cantonal bank. The Rassemblement also formed its own youth organization, *Les Béliers* (the rams), which organized pockets of separatist sentiment in a number of Jurassian communes. Although the tactics employed by the FLJ aroused disapproval in both French and German Switzerland, its extremist activities succeeded in drawing considerable attention to the French-speaking minority in the Jura, both in Switzerland and abroad.

Meanwhile, the Rassemblement, while not participating in the violence, took advantage of the publicity. As Reymond (1965) points out, this turn of events enabled the Rassemblement to build up a disciplined mass following in the Jura that was too strong to be ignored or bypassed in a search for a solution. As the Jurassian organizations continued to grow, Bernese officials once again were forced to reevaluate the Jura problem. In 1967 cantonal authorities formed a *Committee of 24* whose task it was to investigate all aspects of the problem (Kommission der 24, 1968). A little over a year later, the Bernese government announced that it would submit the question of creating a separate canton for the Jura to a plebiscite of voters in the Jura alone. This procedure, which required an amendment to the Bernese constitution, was accepted in March 1970 by 90 percent of the electorate in the Jura and 85 percent in the old canton of Bern. It opened the way for a whole series of referenda that allowed the electorate of the Jura full rights of determination as to the creation of a new canton.

In the first referendum, in June 1974, a slight majority of the Jura population decided to form their own canton. Under the constitutional amendment, any of the six Francophone districts that found themselves opposed to the majority decision were given the opportunity to indicate in a second referendum whether they wanted to secede or to stay with the canton of Bern. In March 1975 another vote was taken, in which the southern French-speaking Protestant districts of Courtelary, Moutier, and La Neuveville decided to remain with the canton of Bern (see Figure 4). In September 1975, border communes dissenting from the rest of their district were able to decide whether they wanted to remain with their old district or join one of their own persuasion. The German-speaking Catholic district of Laufen, with the creation of the new canton of Jura, is physically separated from the old canton. Laufen voted on March 16, 1980, to seek attachment to Basel-Land, by a margin of 30 percent over the canton of Solothurn. The vote was 65 percent for Basel-Land as opposed to 35 percent for Solothurn (*Tages-Anzeiger*, foreign edition, Zurich,

Figure 4. Location of Cantons Bern and Jura with Jura districts.

March 18, 1980). A final decision between remaining with Bern or attaching to Basel-Land will be the subject of a final balloting. The final step in the creation of a new canton of Jura took place on September 24, 1978, when, after years of turmoil, the Swiss populace voted to change Article 2 of the Federal Constitution, which enumerates the cantons, in order to add the canton of Jura. It officially came into existence on January 1, 1979.

The new canton was accepted by over 82 percent of the voting populace. That the Italian-speaking canton of Ticino, the French-speaking cantons of Geneva, Vaud, and Neuchâtel, and the predominantly bilingual (French and German) cantons of Valais and Fribourg overwhelmingly passed the referendum, is perhaps less surprising than the result in a large number of German-speaking cantons, where the vote ran more than 80 percent in favor of the new canton (see Table 24). The fact that Bern figures at the bottom of the list is largely due to the vote of the anti-separatist forces in South Jura. In the three South Jura districts of Moutier, Courtelary, and La Neuveville, there were 12,611 no votes against 11,898 yes votes to turn down the new canton of Jura.

TABLE 24. Results of the Jura vote
(September 24, 1978)

Canton	Percentage of yes votes
Ticino	95.1%
Valais	91.9
Geneva	91.2
Fribourg	90.1
Obwalden	89.3
Vaud	88.6
Lucerne	88.5
Zug	87.1
Appenzell Inner Rhoden	87.0
Nidwalden	86.5
Basel-Stadt	86.0
Schwyz	85.9
Uri	85.4
Basel-Land	84.9
Neuchâtel	84.7
St. Gallen	83.0
Grisons	82.9
Zurich	82.4
Thurgau	81.1
Glarus	80.6
Aargau	80.2
Solothurn	80.1
Schaffhausen	79.2
Appenzell Outer Rhoden	73.1
Bern	69.6
All Switzerland	82.3%

Source: *Neue Zürcher Zeitung*, Sept. 25, 1978.

What stands out above all in the Jura conflict is its particularly un-Swiss flavor of ultranationalism and a degree of ethnic confrontation practically unknown in modern Switzerland. Ernst (1954:6, 29) observes that "The bitter uncompromising campaign of the Jurassian separatists . . . is an experience which, against the background of our [Swiss] ingrained political concept of tolerance, must appear a breakdown of the most painful kind." The Rassemblement was quick to develop a concept of intense self-conscious nationalism—symbolized in the mystique of the *"âme jurassienne"*—which included overtones of ethnic oppression and a united action of French Switzerland to resist German Swiss pressures. Such doctrines had hardly been heard in Switzerland since the threats of Pan-Germanism prior to World War I (McRae, 1964 and 1978). On the other hand, the Bernese authorities were slow to recognize the intricate issues of Jura nationalism.[3] They made few attempts to insure that Jurassians did not feel themselves permanently disadvantaged within the canton.

Nonetheless, it is important that outside the canton the issue acquired few ethnic overtones. In general, the Rassemblement received a wary reception in the rest of French Switzerland. Gonzague de Reynold (1968) insisted that the Jura problem was primarily one of the capacity of the Jura to form its own canton, rather than being based on language or ethnicity.

While the separatists did gain a considerable amount of attention, some of their demands could hardly be seriously considered. Prior to the vote of June 1974, in which the Rassemblement at last cooperated, it demanded that all nonresident Jurassians living elsewhere in Switzerland be allowed to vote, and all "non-genuine" Jurassians—in practice, German-speaking residents—be excluded. Of course, no democratic regime could possibly agree to an electoral roll of that kind.

In the six months after the 1974 plebiscite, the anti-separatist youth movement sprang into life. The *Sangliers* (the wild boars) promised to meet the *Beliers* head-on, in language too tragically redolent of Northern Ireland. The worst violence came after the March 1975 plebiscite. In a close vote, Moutier narrowly elected to remain with the old canton of Bern (the vote was 2,524 for remaining in Bern, and 2,238 for joining the new canton of Jura). Sentiments polarized, and on April 24th a demonstration of *Beliers*

3. For example, the canton of Bern failed to take into account the special needs and sentiments of the francophone Catholic inhabitants of the Jura mountains, who felt threatened by an influx of German-speakers to the northern Jura (Warburton, 1976).

in Moutier got out of hand. There were no fatalities, but ten policemen were seriously injured.

Moutier remains the most polarized of the southern Jura districts. At a meeting of the Rassemblement jurassien in September 1979, Roland Béguelin, who had earlier launched a widespread, bitter attack on the Swiss political system as a system of ethnic domination (1973), demanded that Moutier be allowed to join the canton of Jura. He estimated that the separatists (who are over-represented among the young) would comprise a majority in less than eight years. The almost equal numbers between pro- and anti-Jura forces makes the situation in the South Jura at times tense. While many Swiss politicians and social observers are concerned about the continued militance of both the Rassemblement jurassien and anti-Jurassian forces in the South Jura, the conflict has remained at the local level.

In tracing the roots of the Jura question, no simple explanation is possible. The separatist phenomenon is related to multiple factors, including a combination of linguistic and religious characteristics, religious and political minorization, economic and political marginality, and a centuries-old myth of a Jura state. Of obvious importance also has been a dedicated human element with an unswerving commitment to Jurassian autonomy (McRae, 1978).

The attempts toward resolution of the Jura situation have been influenced by a number of features which contribute to the Swiss political reality. The first is the way the Swiss structure of politics acts to focus on ever smaller and more precise geographical units. The series of referenda described above were designed to give full expression to the popular will. The separation issue was tested, subject only to practical limits, down to the level of the smallest commune. Second is the peculiar flexibility of Swiss constitutions. Unlike the United States Constitution, which is very difficult to amend, Swiss constitutions, both cantonal and federal, can be altered if circumstances require it. An amendment to the Bernese constitution which was accepted by the voters in 1970 made it possible for Jura citizens to demand a vote on separatism. Finally, there is the Swiss spirit of accommodation, which is intertwined with cantonal autonomy and a particularistic Swiss identity. This identity is based on the preservation of the smallest ethnic, linguistic, and cultural units. Because most Swiss are devoted to local autonomy, they were inclined to the view that if the Jurassians themselves want a separate canton, they should have it.

In a broader comparative perspective, the Jura situation sheds light on two important aspects of pluralistic nations. First, it demonstrates that even Switzerland, which is a model of long-lasting coexistence among cantons of socioeconomic, linguistic, and religious diversity, may also be plagued by ethnic troubles. The latent possibility for ethnic conflict is always inherent in societies that are composed of more than one ethnic group. More important, however, Switzerland provides one of the few examples where a solution is at hand among what Bassand (1975) calls "nationalitarian movements," i.e., movements based on a search for identity and a more or less clearly defined desire for autonomy and secession.

Of primary importance in working out a solution was the adaptability of the political system. The Swiss have tended to see politics as simply a process for working out common-sense solutions. Thus political life in Switzerland, including the operation of federal and communal politics, is more flexible than in many countries. We have seen the relative ease with which the Bernese constitution was amended in order to give full expression to the popular will. In addition, the Jura question, unlike most nationalitarian problems, may be dealt with by dusting off an old technique of conflict resolution, rather than by having to create a new pattern. The solution to the Jura conflict, the creation of a new canton (or half-canton, a solution which was also briefly considered) is one of the oldest conflict-resolution techniques in Swiss history (Dunn, 1972). Of obvious importance is also the willingness of the elite and the populace to forge and undertake viable political solutions. After much hesitation, both Bernese and federal officials attempted to seek a workable compromise. In these respects, the situation in the Jura illuminates both the failings and the successes of cultural coexistence in Switzerland.

The *Gastarbeiter* Problem

The foreign-worker problem is more intractable than the Jura question. For unlike national minorities, which are continuously accommodated within the political system, the foreign workers stand outside the political system. They are a voiceless minority without the rights of Swiss citizens.

In order to understand the foreign-worker problem in Switzerland, it is necessary to put it into a broader Western European perspective. There are approximately 8 million foreign workers currently employed in Western Europe, accompanied by 4 to 5 million dependents. More than four-fifths of these migrants are residents in West Germany, France, the United Kingdom, and Switzerland; the rest have migrated to Holland, Belgium, Sweden, and Austria. All the receiving societies have experienced rapid economic growth which has proceeded almost unabated since World War II. At the same time, the countries of southern Europe —Greece, Italy, Portugal, Spain, Turkey, and Yugoslavia—as well as two northern countries, Finland and Ireland, have experienced serious unemployment and underemployment. These eight countries have provided approximately three-fourths of the foreign labor employed in Western Europe, the remainder coming from the former colonial territories of France and Britain (Mayer, 1975: 442).

The vast migration of labor into the industrialized countries of Western Europe may be seen as part of the rural-urban migration which has fueled the industrialization of Western Europe for over a century. Indeed, in 1914 foreigners made up 15.4 percent of the resident population in Switzerland, only slightly less than in 1974, when they reached a new peak at 16.5 percent (see Table 25). While all receiving nations in Western Europe have, in recent years, become dependent on foreign labor, no other country is as dependent upon foreign manpower as Switzerland. In 1975, 20 percent of the Swiss labor force (excluding seasonal workers and border crossers), as compared to 11 percent in France, 10 percent in Germany, and 8 percent in the United Kingdom, was composed of foreign workers (Werner, 1977:301).

Switzerland, like the other labor-importing nations of Western Europe, does not think of itself as a nation of immigrants in the traditional sense. Neither it nor the other countries anticipated the coming waves of migrants. On the contrary, at the end of World War II, most experts believed that Western Europe would not be able to provide employment for its own population. When full employment was reached in Switzerland after World War II, this was regarded as a temporary phenomenon, as were the labor shortages that prevailed in the fifties. For this reason, efforts were made to limit the influx of foreigners to single young males, or those without families, so they could easily be sent home if economic conditions deteriorated.

Since then, even though Western Europe and Switzerland, in particular, have become permanently dependent upon the presence of foreign labor for the functioning of crucial sectors of their economy, the self-image of Western European countries has not basically changed. Mayer (1975:443) observes:

The very terms employed in the current debate prove this point: the discussion is always about guest workers, never about immigrants. Large sections of the Western European public refuse to accept the idea that the foreigners in their midst could become permanent settlers. Any government that was to set out openly to invite foreigners to settle permanently on purely economic grounds would be voted out of office.[4]

TABLE 25. Foreign resident population in Switzerland, 1850-1978[a]

Year	Number	Percentage of total population	Year	Number	Percentage of total population
1850	71,970	3.0%	1966	844,987[b]	14.2%
1860	114,983	4.6	1967	890,580[b]	14.8
1870	150,907	5.7	1968	933,142[b]	15.3
1880	211,035	7.4	1969	971,795[b]	15.7
1888	229,650	7.9	1970	982,887[b]	15.9
1900	383,424	11.6	1971	999,309[b]	15.9
1910	552,011	14.7	1972	1,032,285[b]	16.2
1914	600,000	15.4	1973	1,052,505[b]	16.4
1920	402,385	10.4	1974	1,064,526[b]	16.5
1930	355,522	8.7	1975	1,012,710[b]	15.8
1941	223,554	5.2	1976	958,599[b]	15.1
1950	285,446	6.1	1977	932,743[b]	14.7
1960	584,739	10.8	1978	898,062[b]	14.2
1965	810,243[b]	13.8			

[a]The foreign "resident population" is made up of foreigners with a permanent residence permit and foreigners with a yearly permit.

[b]Not included in these figures are members of international organizations and their families.

Sources: Hoffmann-Nowotny (1974:3) and *Annuaire Statistique de la Suisse* (1979:16, 90).

4. In contrast to Germany and Switzerland, Sweden attempts to assimilate its foreign labor force, rather than treating them as temporary workers. Oberg (1974:2) comments that "It was and still is out of the question to call these immigrants 'guest' workers" (i.e., *Gastarbeiter*). Consistent with this policy, a work permit in Sweden is not tied to a contractually limited period of employment. After the first year, during which the immigrant is usually restricted to a particular branch of industry, he or she is able to move freely in the labor market. Swedish immigrants may also claim all the social benefits of Swedish citizens.

In Switzerland, the federal government has consistently taken a stand against widespread naturalization. In 1969 it stated that naturalization should not serve as a "decisive means" toward reducing the proportion of foreigners: "The number of naturalizations will and must continue to be small" (*Bericht des Bundesrates*, 1969). The percentage of the foreign resident population being naturalized has rarely exceeded 1 percent. In 1977 it stood at 1.5 percent, and in 1978 it was 1.1 percent (*Volkswirtschaft*, 1979:158). A considerable number of these naturalizations are women married to Swiss men, who automatically obtain Swiss citizenship.[5]

This poses a basic dilemma and represents an obvious shortcoming in the Swiss mode of integration of non-national minorities. While at first the intention of the migrant workers who did not plan to expatriate themselves coincided with the attitudes and intentions of the receiving countries, this situation has become increasingly illusionary. Both the length of stay and the percentage of foreign workers with year-round permits have increased (see Table 26). There has also been a change in the composition of the foreign resident population, with an increasing number of family members joining foreign workers. In 1977, more than a fourth of the foreign resident population were children 16 years and under, many of whom have spent a considerable part of their life in Switzerland. The percentage in this age category increased from 13 to 30 percent between 1960 and 1977.

Further evidence of increasing stabilization and decreasing rotation of the foreign labor force is evident in the rapidly increasing number of aliens who have been given the right of permanent

TABLE 26. *Length of stay of workers with year-round permits*

Date of enumeration	Less than 3 years	3 and more years	5 and more years
October 1955	75%	25%	11%
February 1959	75	25	11
December 1970	40	60	44
December 1977	35	65	41

Source: *Die Volkswirtschaft* 43 (April 1970:157) and 52 (March 1978:137).

5. According to the Swiss law, to become naturalized an immigrant must live in Switzerland for at least 12 years; have been physically present in Switzerland for 3 of the last 5 years; and undergo a federal investigation.

settlement. They have increased from about 4,000 in 1959 to 31,000 in 1970, and to 59,000 in 1977, and will, unless anti-foreign sentiment intensifies, expand still further in the coming years, because of the massive immigration ten years earlier (the time required to obtain permanent residence) in the decade and a half between 1960 and 1975. Thus, given the heavy reliance of Swiss industries on foreign workers and the increasing permanence of this labor force, the Swiss must accommodate themselves to the presence of a large number of foreigners in their midst.

The official policy of the federal government is one of stabilization of the foreign population to a number that would be "politically acceptable" (see Troxler, 1975:14). It is more vague, however, on the "assimilation" of foreigners. The Federal Consultative Committee for the Problems of Foreign Workers presented a program in 1973, but did not proceed beyond suggesting various measures. Five years later, the summary of the Consultative Committee concluded that assimilation was mainly the responsibility of the enterprises, the unions, and the employers' organizations. They are to work primarily through language and vocational education, and to promote active participation in workers' committees (*Tages-Anzeiger*, foreign edition, Zurich, July 31, 1973: 2, and Feb. 21, 1978:3).

Of course, this can only be a stop-gap measure. While the number of foreigners has decreased from a high point in the early 1970s, it will probably stabilize above 10 percent of the resident population. Unless novel solutions are found for the integration and assimilation of foreign workers, and particularly their children, a considerable portion of the population will be excluded from exerting those basic civil rights linked to citizenship. Having a large population of voiceless residents is a dangerous situation for any country.

Until recently, the majority of the foreign labor force in Switzerland came from neighboring countries—Germany, France, Italy, and Austria. In 1860 these four countries accounted for 97.3 percent of the foreign workers; in 1910, 95.2 percent; and in 1960, 87.1 percent. But by 1978 their share had decreased to less than three-fourths. In addition, Switzerland has witnessed a decrease in the proportion of French and German immigrants and an increase in the proportion of Italians—by 1978, they comprised slightly less than 50 percent of the Swiss foreign labor force (*Volkswirtschaft*, 1979:169).

There has also been a change in the social composition of the foreign workforce. Although the majority of the immigrants have always been members of the working class, the proportion has rapidly risen since 1941 (see Table 27). Furthermore, there were in 1978 over 121,000 seasonal workers (so-called *saisonniers*), the majority of whom worked in unskilled or semi-skilled jobs. Thus, the problem of foreign minorities in Switzerland is one of class as well as ethnicity.

Another important aspect of the foreign-worker problem in Switzerland, as well as in the other Western European labor-importing countries, is their distribution in the occupational structure. Several authors have pointed to the concentration of foreign workers in the lowest-paying and lowest-prestige jobs (Hoffmann-Nowotny, 1973; Castles and Kosack, 1973). Girod (1975) concludes that, on the whole, the percentage of foreigners in an industry is in inverse proportion to the advantages offered to them in terms of income, working conditions, and prestige. Hoffmann-Nowotny (1974:8) speaks of the *Ueberschichtung* of the native population and the *Unterschichtung* of the immigrant population: "*Unterschichtung* means that most immigrants occupy the lowest positions available in the social and occupational structures of the immigrant country, where they form a new social stratum at the very bottom of the occupational ladder." On the other hand, massive *Unterschichtung* opens up greater chances of upward mobility for the native population. Between 1950 and 1960, the number of foreigners occupying semi-skilled and unskilled jobs more than doubled (from 12 to 28 percent), while the percentage

TABLE 27. *Foreign work force according to occupations, 1900-1975*

Year	Workers	Employees	Employers and self-employed	Others
1900	70%	10%	16%	4%
1910	65	11	19	5
1920	63	13	20	4
1930	66	13	17	5
1941	60	14	22	4
1950	73	13	11	3
1960	84	11	4	1
1970	80	18	2	1
1975	80	18	2	—

Sources: Hoffmann-Nowotny (1973:49) and *Die Volkswirtshaft* 49 (Feb. 1975).

of Swiss in these job categories decreased from 88 to 72 percent. Although the proportion of those engaged in such low-paying, low-status occupations as hotel and restaurant work, domestic work, and agriculture has declined since 1956, the majority of foreign immigrants are still concentrated in jobs rejected by Swiss citizens (see Table 28). Foreign men are most likely to go into building trades—which, because of job insecurity, the necessity to move around, and the hard working conditions, are avoided by Swiss men—while immigrant women are most likely to work in the textile industry, which because of low pay and job conditions is similarly rejected by Swiss women.[6]

In Switzerland (as well as France and Germany; see Rist, 1979) the labor unions have taken an ambiguous stand on the incorporation of foreign workers into the labor force. While officially, most unions have special functionaries or committees dealing with foreign workers, unofficially they have not always pushed the organization of foreigners, for a number of reasons. These include economic problems such as the effect on productivity; social ones like the difficulties of integrating large numbers of foreigners; political fears connected with the presence of masses of second-class citizens not owing their loyalty to the Swiss state,

TABLE 28. Distribution of foreign workers by major occupational group, 1956-1970

Major occupational group	1956	1964	1970
Construction, stone, and glass	28.0%	31.6%	27.8%
Metals and machinery	12.7	19.2	19.0
Hotels and restaurants	15.6	10.5	11.5
Textiles and clothing	9.0	11.3	10.1
Professions and arts	3.0	4.2	5.6
Commerce	1.2	3.9	5.2
Private households	11.6	3.4	3.7
Food, beverages, and tobacco	2.7	3.5	3.4
Agriculture	10.5	2.5	2.2
Other occupations	5.7	9.9	11.5
Total	100.0%	100.0%	100.0%

Source: *Die Volkwirtschaft* 43 (April 1970: 556).

6. For a detailed study of the position of female foreign workers in Switzerland, see Ley (1979).

the radicalization of workers with Communist leanings, difficulties for the trade unions arising out of conflict with Swiss workers, and the unwillingness of foreign workers to join Swiss unions (Castles and Kosack, 1973:147; Dubs, 1970:3-4).

While the massive movement of foreigners into the Swiss labor market has increased the mobility rates of Swiss workers into the ranks of manual and white-collar jobs, it has also deprived the unions of part of their traditional membership. White-collar workers, in particular, tend to have low rates of union participation. Similarly, the Socialist Party has observed that the domestic working class and its political influence are slowly eroding. Siegenthaler (1975:276) notes: "These concerns, which are seldomly openly admitted by the S.G.B. (Swiss Trade Union Federation) and S.P. (Social Democratic Party), have contributed to the rising criticism of employing large numbers of foreign workers."

On the other hand, there have been some efforts, particularly by union leaders, to integrate foreign workers into the labor force and trade-union movement. Besides demanding equal pay and conditions for foreign workers, on occasion they have protested against the expulsion of foreign workers because of political and trade-union activity, and demanded recognition of their civil rights. Nevertheless, the xenophobic reactions of many rank-and-file unionists, especially during the hysteria of the early 1970s, have left many foreign workers feeling that the Swiss unions do not represent their interests.

Since Switzerland does not think of the foreign workers as a permanent labor force, there is an absence of a true immigration policy. Instead, one finds an elaborate set of rules governing admission into the country. First a foreigner must obtain a work permit, which—provided he or she does not come as a *saisonnier*—is issued for one year. When the year is up, the permit may be renewed for another one-year period, and after a stay of five years for a two-year period. The immigrant, however, has no legal claim to the prolongation of his permit, which remains at the discretion of the authorities. Furthermore, the foreigner needs special permission to move to another canton or change jobs. In 1973, the number of years of service required before a foreign worker could change jobs or work-places was decreased from five to two years. Finally, after a stay of ten years and a federal investigation, the immigrant is granted a resident permit, which gives him equal rights in the job market with Swiss citizens (Hoffmann-Nowotny, 1974:14-15). At this time he is also normally entitled to unemployment benefits.

Other restrictions on the rights of foreigners are applied with respect to their families. A foreigner who is obliged to reapply each year for a new permit is allowed to have his family join him only after he has spent one year in Switzerland. In order to do this, he must provide proof that he has obtained adequate living quarters and that he is financially capable of supporting them. Housing may not, however, be obtained at the expense of Swiss nationals (Hoffmann-Nowotny, 1974:15-16).

Despite some recent attempts to make concessions to foreign workers now in Switzerland in areas such as family policy and geographical and job mobility, the foreign population continues to be politically voiceless. They are denied the rights of political participation, including an appeals process against job dismissal and deportation, and of citizenship for their children, even though they are born and live in Switzerland until adolescence.

The absence of political rights, and the lack of consensus about the nature of Swiss immigration, is particularly debilitating for the children of foreign workers. Although it is a generally unexpressed understanding that immigration is a temporary phenomenon, the Swiss educational system has ordinarily held that the children of foreigners should be prepared for longer-term residence. Thus they usually attend the same schools and follow the same curriculum as Swiss children. However, in addition to the regular subjects, some foreign children also receive instruction in their mother tongue. This places an extra burden on these children, who too often have an insufficient knowledge of both the national language and their native tongue.

Hoffmann-Nowotny (1974:19) further observes that:

> While there is no formal discrimination against foreign children, it is easy to understand why they are usually below the standard of native children and rarely succeed in going on to middle or higher education. . . . While in several places there are programs aimed at reducing the disadvantaged position of foreign children, these programs reach only a minority of children. . . . So the assumption that the foreign children will simply grow up to form a new subproletariat, replicating that of their parents today, will probably be confirmed.

The double insecurity reflected in the attitudes of the immigrants is referred to by Braun (1970:437) as *Heimkehrillusion* (the illusion of returning home). His extensive survey of four middle-sized towns in German Switzerland shows that a very high percentage of Italians, at the moment of entry, and approximately five years later, have no definite intended length of stay. Generally, there is a strong shift toward an increased time horizon the longer the actual length of stay (Braun, 1970:488). This evidence contradicts the assertions of Swiss (and other Western European) politicians who have maintained that Italian immigrants come with the definite intention of wanting to stay for only a year or two and then to return home.

In recent years, immigration has become one of the most-debated political issues. Pressure from groups campaigning against the foreign domination or overforeignization (*Ueberfremdung*) of the country helped to force through regulations restricting the entry of new foreign workers in 1964 and subsequent years. The campaign against immigrants reached a climax in June 1970, when every male Swiss citizen (women were not enfranchised until 1971) was asked to vote in a referendum on whether the proportion of foreigners should be limited to 10 percent of the population both in the country as a whole and in each canton (with the exception of Geneva). Acceptance of this referendum would have meant the expulsion of a large number of immigrants from Switzerland. The move was sponsored by James Schwarzenbach and opposed by the Federal Council, the trade unions, and all major political parties. Even so, it was only defeated by a modest majority (54 percent) (Petersen, 1975:196).

Two more national referenda were also held on the overforeignization issue. Late in 1972, Schwarzenbach's right-wing party, the *Nationale Aktion für Volk und Heimat* (the National Movement for People and Homeland), began to collect signatures for an even more drastic proposal. Under its terms, there would have been a sharp reduction in the number of foreigners—two out of every five would have been expelled by 1978. The referendum came to a vote in 1974, and was defeated by about two to one. Since then, for the third time, the Swiss citizens have turned down an "Ueberfremdungsinitiative" in 1977—this time by an even more decisive 71 percent. The Schwarzenbach initiatives are indicative of the mood of the country.[7] What seems to have been the issue, more than the economic question of whether foreign workers held back or contributed to growth, was the threat to the Swiss way of life and "Swissness" that a large Catholic Italian-speaking population, lacking Swiss traditions and habits, posed for the delicately balanced Swiss society (Kindleberger, 1967:46).

7. Even though the initiatives were turned down, many foreign workers were forced to leave Switzerland during 1974-1976 in the course of the recession. Critics have charged that Switzerland's low jobless rate (ranging from 1-2 percent —one of the lowest in the world) is largely the result of exporting unemployment abroad.

Traditionally, the coexistence among French-, German-, and Italian-speaking Swiss, as well as between Catholic and Protestant Swiss, has rested on the stable proportions of the major language and religious groups, which have persisted with only minor variations for well over a century. The foreigners could change this balance. For example, in 1970, 80.0 percent of the aliens, but only 43.4 percent of Swiss citizens, gave their religion as Catholic. According to the same census, the respective percentages of Swiss citizens and aliens speaking the country's main languages were as follows: German, 74.5 and 19.1 percent; French, 20.1 and 8.2 percent; and Italian, 4.0 and 49.7 percent (Mayer, 1977). Italian, which was once more or less limited to the canton of Ticino, has become an important second language, especially in the cities of German Switzerland, where many of the immigrants work. In accordance with the principle of territoriality, if the immigrants are allowed to stay, they and particularly their children will adapt to the language of the area. Thus the large immigration of Italians which has reduced German-speaking residents to their lowest proportion in Swiss history may eventually have the contrary effect of reinforcing the German-language group at the expense of French. Therefore, in the long run, the integration of immigrants may be the real testing-ground for Swiss coexistence.

6 | Reflections on Diversity in Switzerland

After looking at some of the current unsettled questions of linguistic and ethnic tensions in Switzerland today, one must return to the factors making for stability and adjustment within the existing political system. We began this work by observing that among linguistically fragmented states, Switzerland is one of the few examples of a country whose overall political unity is not threatened. It is a well-established proposition, reaching back at least as far as Aristotle, that self-governing polities face implicit obstacles in so-called "plural societies"—that is, societies with clearly discernible racial, linguistic, and religious differences.

In order to explain the apparent Swiss anomaly, many social observers have relied heavily on structural factors. The hypothesis of cross-cutting cleavages has been applied to Switzerland, at least superficially, by many scholars. Currently it represents one of the dominant views of Swiss society. The fundamental error committed by cross-cutting theorists is to reduce and simplify the complex interaction of groups to certain aspects of social structure. Mayer, for instance, attributes the general civic harmony in Switzerland to its unique social characteristics. Furthermore, he notes that in the one instance, the Jura, where these conditions are absent, conflict occurs. He states (Mayer, 1968:707) that:

> The Swiss "miracle" of unity in diversity rests upon a peculiar equilibrium of cross-cutting cultural divisions which is historically unique and cannot be duplicated under different conditions. Interestingly, and largely unknown to the outside world, Switzerland itself furnishes proof that if the divisions between the linguistic and religious groups do not overlap, but coincide, the result is conflict instead of harmony.

147

For Mayer, the conflict situation in the Jura serves as a confirmation of the salience of the cross-cutting hypothesis. While he points out that the purpose of his article is "neither prediction nor advocacy," there are, paradoxically, undertones in his analysis of an almost deterministic belief in the explosive potential of what he terms "cultural divisions." This tendency is evident in his mechanical and abstract manner of applying the cross-cutting hypothesis. Peaceful coexistence is seen primarily as a function of certain characteristics of social structure which he summarizes (1968:714-720) as follows:

> First, and perhaps foremost, is the fact that the linguistic boundaries do not coincide with but cross-cut across the religious boundaries. . . . [Second is] the fact that the dividing lines between the languages do not coincide for the most part with the cantonal boundaries, . . . [and third] the fact that economic differences do not coincide with linguistic boundaries.

Public policy and the political art, as well as other factors such as religious and ideological differences expressed in the party system and the political process, are of secondary importance in Mayer's analysis.

By itself, the cross-cutting hypothesis seems insufficient to explain Swiss coexistence. Why do the Murteners not attempt to separate from the canton of Fribourg? Like the Catholic, French-speaking Jurassians, they occupy a double-minority status in the canton—they are Protestant and German-speaking in a predominantly Catholic and French-speaking canton—and were annexed to a canton against their will. In addition, both French- and German-speaking Swiss observers have noted that the German-speaking minority in Fribourg has been the most disadvantaged linguistic group in all of Switzerland (Pichard, 1975:184-191; Allemann, 1968:373-374). Still, there is no longer any separatism (some attempts were made to separate from Fribourg and join Bern, with whom it shares its religion and language, in the nineteenth century) and certainly no violence. It seems unlikely that we can attribute this difference in behavior exclusively to the fact that the Murtener is part of a religious and linguistic majority in the nation, although a double minority in the canton, while prior to the formation of the new canton of Jura the North Jurassian was part of a double ethnic minority in both canton and nation.

The Jura conflict illustrates yet a further limitation of the cross-cutting hypothesis. Even though the Catholic, French-speaking citizens of the Jura occupied a cumulative minority position in the canton of Bern and the Confederation, the Jura district of Bern itself appeared to offer a classic example of cross-cutting cleavages, with almost 24 percent of its residents speaking German and 41 percent of the population adhering to the Protestant faith. Moreover, prior to the formation of the canton of Jura, three of the six French-speaking districts in the area were mainly Protestant and three were mainly Catholic (Kommission der 24, 1968:92-101). The seventh district was overwhelmingly German-speaking and Catholic. As one Swiss political scientist (Reymond, 1965:36) has observed:

> In the Jura, neither political particularisms nor the distribution of languages explains or justifies a separatist movement; it would seem rather that the extreme overlapping of tongues, the relative equilibrium of religions . . . ought to lead the different groups to agreement.

As we have seen, this has not been the case. Cross-cutting cleavages do not eliminate polar-opposite groups, but merely reduce their size relative to groups halfway in between, in this case German Catholics and French Protestants. Thus, if one assumes that French Catholics are not only the most separatist but also have been the source of most of the violent acts, one can note an interesting limitation of the cross-cutting hypothesis. Keech (1972:404) observes that "Since it does not take more than a handful of people to commit the acts of violence which make ethnic conflict in the Jura 'intense,' cross-cutting cleavages do not help much to reduce violence." Rather, it is the *perception* of cleavages as congruent which can reinforce the self-consciousness of ethnic groups. This opens up a series of difficult questions about the relative salience and intensity of cleavages and perception of cleavages which is rarely asked by adherents of the cross-cutting hypothesis (see McRae, 1975).

The model of consociational democracy, although contributing to an explanation of Swiss stability, also leaves many issues unsolved. By emphasizing the conscious and deliberate efforts of autonomous elite politics it neglects the role of popular sentiment and public opinion. Elite accommodation does not mean much if a minority is consistently outvoted and forced to bend to the desires of the majority. In fact, elite accommodation seems to be possible only in those societies where there is substantial agreement among the citizenry and its leaders on a common civic culture.

A Portrait of Swiss Intergroup Relations

In order to explore the salience of popular sentiment and public opinion in contributing to Swiss coexistence, our study has concentrated on the transmission of values in a multicultural setting. We have made a distinction between official institutions, whose task it is to socialize the general public, and the values reported by the populace itself. To address the first question, the role of the school and its curriculum was examined.

An investigation of Swiss history textbooks from French and German, Catholic and Protestant Switzerland was particularly revealing. In contrast to Canada and South Africa, the school curriculum tends to unite rather than to divide the various cultural groups, by deemphasizing those historical themes which feed intergroup resentment. The textbooks instill a sense of national consciousness. Even though the authors present various interpretations of some events, there is an underlying consensus of what the Swiss state should stand for. One may even hypothesize that there has gradually evolved in Switzerland a civic culture comparable to the civil religion[1] in the United States. Herberg (1955) and Bellah (1967) have contended that the mutual toleration among Protestants, Catholics, and Jews in America is possible because they all, majority and minority alike, participate in a common civil religion. The American civil religion celebrates "the American Way of Life." Since it does not align itself with any particular religious theology, and since it was never anti-clerical or militantly secular, the civil religion was able, without any bitter struggle with the church, to build up powerful symbols of national solidarity and to mobilize deep levels of personal motivation for the attainment of national goals.

Likewise, it appears that Switzerland's linguistic and religious minorities participate in a common "civic culture." This does not mean that all differences among the groups have disappeared. But

---

1. Rousseau, who coined the term "civil religion," meant by it the "purely civil profession of faith, whose articles the sovereign is competent to determine," which induced man to "love his duties." "The dogmas of the civil religion ought to be simple, few, and precisely formulated, without explanations or commentaries. The existence of a powerful, intelligent, benevolent, foreseeing, and providential God, the continuance of life after death, the happiness of the just, the punishment of the wicked, the sanctity of the social contract and the laws, these are the positive dogmas. As for the negative dogmas, I would limit them to one only, namely intolerance" (Rousseau, 1953:153).

Lincoln's use of the term "political religion" constituted by "reverence for the laws" is identical to Rousseau's usage (see Jaffa, 1959:227).

it does indicate that the various groups have learned to accept their differences by and large, and those differences, be they religious, linguistic, or cultural, are moderated by other things the groups have in common. This interpretation is strengthened when we turn to the results of our survey of French- and German-speaking youth. Political reasons were given considerably more often than any other reasons when Swiss youth were asked why they were proud to be Swiss. Even before they reach adulthood, young people seem to have a "certain Swiss outlook."

Majority opinion also plays a special role in Swiss cultural coexistence. While the French Swiss youth display many indicators of what might be called a typical minority response—such as their greater perception of dissent among different Swiss subgroups, their preference for the cantonal over the federal government, their desire to live in a territory where they predominate, and their reservations about their homeland (almost one-fourth said they were not particularly proud to be Swiss)—the German Swiss do not display a parallel "majoritarian attitude." An interesting indication of the nonmajoritarian attitude of the German Swiss majority can be seen in their approximations of the three Swiss language communities. The German Swiss underestimate their own numbers in the population and overestimate the linguistic minorities, while in general the opposite tendency is true of the French Swiss, who overestimate themselves and underestimate the German-speaking population. Linguistic harmony among the German-, French-, and Italian-language communities is certainly fostered by this balance, which favors the smaller groups.

Other factors influence the Swiss panorama of intergroup relations. Ethnic integration in multicultural states can take a whole range of alternatives, from complete lack of official recognition of ethnic identity by the state to a full-blown official acceptance of the communal principle. In the first case, the state merely recognizes territorial divisions and incorporates its citizens as individuals, without giving ethnic identity any legal status whatsoever. In the latter case, the state incorporates its citizens as members of officially recognized ethnic communities. Thus the recognition of ethnicity is legally built into the structure of representation. Switzerland may be cited as an example of the first type of arrangement,[2] and Belgium and Yugoslavia as examples of the second. As Van den Berghe (1976:253) remarks:

2. It may also be argued that Switzerland is a federation of political communities and cantons, and incorporates its citizens first and foremost at this level, rather than as individuals or ethnic groups.

In practical terms, a Swiss-type solution based on territorial divisions without formal recognition of ethnicity by the state is preferable to, say, a Belgian-type solution. Territoriality allows the application of a simple unambiguous test of membership such as a place of residence. Such a criterion gives every citizen a formally equal place, even when he chooses to live in the territory of another ethnic group. Certain regions may be *de facto* the turf of a given ethnic group, but the state gives no *de jure* recognition to ethnicity as such.

The incorporation of citizens as individuals rather than as members of officially recognized ethnic groups serves to deemphasize ethnicity, as well as to reaffirm the principle of legal equality of individuals so as to offer no points of collision with the foundation of the modern democratic state.

The strict application of the territorial principle in the area of language usage has led to another condition which has promoted linguistic harmony. In Switzerland there exist three separate linguistic melting pots—French, Italian, and German. Coupled with demographic trends which tend to stabilize the relative proportions of the three language groups, and the relatively rapid assimilation of new migrants, the Latin groups are able to be masters in their own homes without the threat of Germanization.[3] Two further factors which add to the resilience of the Swiss linguistic melting-pots are the substantial economic equality among the three language communities, and the international prestige of French, Italian, and German.

Public policy also favors the linguistic minorities. Von Greyerz (1959:178-179) argues that the Swiss are willing to overrepresent minorities rather than possibly deprive them of representation. This is true of political parties, which attempt to balance ethnic representation, as well as of proportionally staffed government agencies. The process of decision-making, like that of representation, seeks practical compromise solutions to which all parties agree in the end—what is commonly referred to as "*Echt eidgenössischer Kompromiss.*" This attitude, which emphasizes the accommodation of differences, can be observed in such diverse places as Swiss textbooks and government documents. Despite continued

3. The influx of German-speakers, both from Germany and German Switzerland, has been a greater threat in the Ticino, especially in the scenic areas around Lucarno and Lugano, than in French Switzerland. After a period of acute cultural tension in the first three decades of the twentieth century, assimilation of German-speaking youth appears to be progressing more rapidly today. Many of the immigrants, however, remain economically superior to the native Ticinese (see McRae, 1964:61-65).

animosity by some French-speaking Jurassians toward the predominantly German-speaking canton of Bern, the cantonal committee, composed of both French- and German-speakers, prefaced
their report with a statement (Kommission der 24, 1968:2) emphasizing the need for compromise among all participants:

> This attitude [of compromise], which implies respect for minorities,
> means that it is not the numerical strength of the group that should
> be decisive, with an individual being placed at a disadvantage merely
> because he is a member of a minority group.

Thus, in Switzerland we find not only acceptance of, but also a
commitment to, interethnic equality.

Theoretical and Practical Implications for Other Countries

Are there any matters in which other multicultural nations
may profit from the Swiss experience? Bryce (1921:502, 499)
warns us that:

> To create the moral and intellectual conditions that have formed the
> political character of the [Swiss] people would be, if possible at all, a
> difficult and extremely slow work. . . . Where an institution has suc-
> ceeded with one particular people and in one set of economic condi-
> tions, the presumption that it will suit another people living under
> different conditions is a weak presumption and affords slight basis
> for prediction.

Despite the difficulty of transferring attitudes and institutions,
and the imperfections in Swiss policy and practice, Switzerland's
experience appears to point to a variety of conditions which foster
stable and effective democracy in countries with discernible linguistic, religious, and cultural differences.

The prospects for democratic pluralism appear closely related
to the degree of consensus about basic values. The existence of a
civic culture moderates social conflicts and promotes stability in
multicultural societies. However, substantial agreement between
cultural groups does not prevent occasional disruptions of hostility, such as is the case in the Jura. Nevertheless, where value
consensus exists in heterogeneous societies, the chances for peaceful resolution of differences are considerably improved.

In addition to value consensus, democratic pluralism seems to
be greatly aided by an acceptance and commitment to cultural
pluralism. Van den Berghe (1971b:76) observes that this includes
"both more general norms accepting the legitimacy of pluralism

and more specific counteracculturative norms ensuring the continued integrity of the group." The overemphasis on assimilation by students of ethnicity in the United States has obscured the distinction between transitory pluralism—where immigrant groups, though they may be sizable, self-conscious, and organized, become assimilated within two or three generations (e.g., the Irish or Italians in the United States)[4]—and stable pluralism, a situation in which groups, especially ethnic groups, preserve their separate identity and resist assimilation for many generations (e.g., the French and Italians in Switzerland, and the French in Quebec).[5]

It appears that in the emerging third-world countries, as well as in the first and second worlds, stable pluralism, rather than transitory pluralism, will have to be recognized and addressed in government policies. Recent ethnic outbreaks throughout the world have testified to the fact that ethnicity is not "withering away," and that it will be a permanent feature of most countries for the foreseeable future. Where ethnic groups are territorially concentrated, cultural and regional autonomy will need to be explored as mechanisms for intergroup-conflict resolution. Other important issues are the use and status of various languages and the control and nature of formal education. These questions are often interconnected with linguistic and/or religious preservation and identity. According to Van den Berghe (1971a:517):

> The challenge is to recognize the legitimacy of cultural pluralism; to accommodate local demands for limited autonomy; to protect people's wishes to speak their own language, practice their own religion, and live out their lives in the cultural medium of their choice; and at the same time to preserve the political integrity of the states which will have to be multinational if they are to be viable at all.

In addition to these two factors, the successful operation of democratic pluralism seems to be related to a consensus about procedural norms of the government which result in an equitable division of power between ethnic groups. In Switzerland, this is achieved by a grand coalition of the political leaders of all the communities into which the society is divided, and application of the principle of proportionality both for the election of parliaments and the allocation of civil service and military appoint-

---

4. Most policies concerning ethnic minorities in the United States, such as affirmative action and civil rights, are conceived as aiding the assimilation of oppressed minorities rather than preserving their identity.

5. The distinction between transitory and stable pluralism is made by Van den Berghe (1971b).

ments. Beyond these positive mechanisms which ensure that the distribution of power in the society is roughly proportional to the size of the various groups, the referendum and initiative also provide a check on the majority. Thus, successful democratic pluralism depends on minorities' being continually accommodated within the political system.

Finally, successful ethnic coexistence is dependent on a significant amount of equality between groups. To the extent that the rapid multiplication and intensification of contacts do create interethnic tensions, these tensions are likely to be aggravated by an awareness of significant inequalities among ethnic groups. Lijphart (1977b:57) makes the distinction between horizontal and vertical ethnic groups, observing that ethnic groups can be defined in terms of their relationship to the economic, status, and power dimensions:

> Vertical groups cut across these dimensions at right angles, whereas the boundaries of horizontal groups coincide with them. Vertical groups are completely equal to each other in terms of class, status, and power; horizontal groups show the highest degree of inequality. In reality, ethnic groups are never purely vertical or purely horizontal, but may be said to approximate one or the other of the two types.

In general, vertical groups are less likely to come into conflict with each other than horizontal groups. Certain conditions, however, appear to foster "resurgent nationalisms" even among roughly equal groups. A notable feature of ethnic confrontations by the French Canadians in Quebec, the Walloons and Flemings in Belgium, the Scots and Welsh in Great Britain, and the Jurassians in Switzerland[6] has been the rising levels of affluence, education, and political potential of the mobilizing minorities (Enloe, 1973). Williams (1979:27) observes that:

> In nearly all the cases, the agitation for ethnic mobilization has been led by a cultural elite that emphasizes an ethnic distinctiveness that would redound to the benefit of members of that elite should it become the basis of political authority or influence.

---

6. In contrast to the more vertical position occupied by the Jurassians, the newly immigrated foreign workers in Switzerland (as well as in the other labor-importing countries of Western Europe) stand at the bottom of the economic, status, and power dimensions of the society. The presence of a highly visible immigrant group, excluded from legitimate political activity and socially and economically inferior to the national population, may in the end pose the greater danger to national stability.

Nevertheless, this should not obscure the fact that there are marked and consistent differences between societies that experience high levels of ethnic violence and societies that have less frequent and less severe ethnic violence. In his study of 19 societies with stable and salient cleavages between a majority and one or more minorities, Hewitt (1977) found that the violent societies showed considerable economic and political inequality, while the societies with low violence were characterized by demographic stability and approximate economic parity among ethnic groups. In addition, there were marked political differences: in the societies low in violence, the minorities were politically well-represented or had substantial territorial autonomy within a federal system.

Cultural Pluralism, Democracy, and the Swiss Case

A basic premise of this work is that viable democratic governments are possible in countries with a fragmented culture. In recent years, democratic pessimists have too readily equated cultural diversity with ethnic confrontation. Fellow feelings can exist in plural societies among people who speak different languages and practice different religions. In this connection, the case of Switzerland offers us important insights into the relationship between heterogeneous states and cultural and ethnic coexistence. Despite its heterogeneity, Switzerland has been able to establish a common "civic culture" that transcends cultural and ethnic boundaries, and provides a foundation for toleration between Swiss linguistic and religious minorities and majorities. In addition, many institutional arrangements have also aided Switzerland's four related language groups of greatly unequal size to achieve a stable and relatively amicable confederation of cantons. These include a grand coalition of the political leaders of all the major communities into which Switzerland is divided, and proportionality both for the election of parliaments and the allocation of civil-service appointments. Buttressing these institutional arrangements are a considerable degree of regional autonomy and economic equality between linguistic groups, as well as a recognition of the legitimacy of cultural pluralism.

Recent decades have shown both the persistence and the resurgence of ethnic politics and confrontation in many societies around the world. Heisler (1977:1) claims that "Ethnic differences are the single most important source of large-scale conflict within states, and they are frequently instrumental in wars between countries as well." Thus it is imperative to explore, with urgency, imagination, and willingness to innovate, just how ethnic differences may be accommodated and reconciled. Neither the United States, with its emphasis on assimilation and majoritarian politics, nor the Soviet Union, which guarantees the right to self-determination of nationalities, including secession, while in practice permitting only formal autonomy and a measure of cultural diversity, currently provide adequate models[7] of ethnic accommodation. Those who set out in the 1980s to reflect upon how ethnic coexistence may be achieved may well find the Swiss experience worthy of study. In the course of history, the Swiss people have come to realize that institutions and sentiments that try to justify themselves by majoritarian principles are not consistent with cultural harmony.

7. Halliday (1979:338-339) observes, "This has been the pattern in the USSR and has been reproduced in Soviet policy towards a number of third world countries where the nationalities issue has come up: in Nigeria, where the Russians backed the suppression of Biafra in the 1960s, in Iraq in 1972-75, where they supported the crushing of the Kurds, and most recently, in Ethiopia, where Russian arms and advisors have been used in the offensive against the Eritreans in 1978."

Appendix I.

Research Procedure and Design

Our questionnaire was designed to investigate young people's attitudes toward diversity in Switzerland, and more generally to record their perceptions about the nature of their country—its people, its culture, its history, and its problems. Approximately half of the questions were designed especially for this study. Both open- and closed-ended questions were drafted to elicit responses about national and subnational alliances, and core values and attitudes. The other half of the survey was either adapted or taken directly from Johnstone's study of *Young People's Images of Canadian Society* (1969). Thus we were able to utilize the Canadian results as a reference point from which to measure the Swiss findings.

The questionnaire was written in English and then translated into French and German. The translations were checked against one another for consistency. Prior to being administered, the questionnaire was pretested on a class of French- and German-speaking Swiss students. A number of secondary-school teachers and students from both linguistic groups made valuable suggestions and corrections in the translation and wording of the questionnaire. The final version in German and French appears in Appendix II.

The survey was given to Swiss students in the last two compulsory grades of secondary school, usually grades 8 and 9, during the months of September and October 1976. The students ranged in age from 14 to 16, with a median age of approximately 15 among both French and German Swiss subgroups. Not surprisingly, considering the multiplicity of school systems in Switzerland, different methods had to be employed to gain entry to the individual classrooms in the various cantons. In some it was sufficient to get permission from the teacher, while in others it was

159

necessary to go through the principal or even the cantonal school authorities. In the majority of cases, the questionnaires were administered by the classroom teacher in my presence. This enabled me to obtain a 100-percent return rate, with the exception of a few absentees. In all, 596 questionnaires were distributed. There were 68 non-Swiss respondents, who were excluded from further evaluation, leaving 538 usable completed questionnaires which were almost evenly divided between French- and German-speakers.

Regional, religious, and linguistic factors were given special attention in the research design. Table A-1 shows the cantons sampled, as well as their linguistic and religious characteristics. Other factors also played a role in the selection of the sample. Since we were primarily interested in the attitudes of the common citizen, we attempted to restrict our survey to what might be called "middle Switzerland," both in terms of class composition of the schools and place of residence. Those areas or cities which would tend to express extremes in attitudes were excluded from consideration. Thus we ommitted the Jura region, which is undoubtedly the most ethnically polarized area of Switzerland, as well as Geneva, which contains the highest percentage of foreigners (over 30 percent) of any Swiss city. On the other hand, in order to compare high- and low-contact areas, we included French and German Swiss students in bilingual cantons with German (Biel/Bienne) and French (Fribourg) majorities.

Coding of Open-Ended Questions

The open-ended questions (nos. 20 and 30), asking Swiss young people why they were proud or not proud to be Swiss, were coded in the following manner. First, approximately 50 randomly selected questionnaires from the two linguistic groups were perused to obtain a general picture of the kinds and number of responses. Approximately 40 categories were established. It was decided to record a maximum of five answers for each subject. Few respondents exceeded this number, and many recorded less than five reasons. If, for example, a subject wrote that he was proud to be Swiss because it was a democratic country, provided for the welfare of the citizen, and was a beautiful country, three responses were coded. In all, 42 categories were elicited as to why they were proud to be Swiss, while 43 categories were established as to why they were not proud to be Swiss. The coding was carried out by

*TABLE A-1. Sample size,[a] by canton,
showing linguistic and religious characteristics*

Canton	City	Number in sample	Characteristics
Vaud	Lausanne	16	French-speaking, formerly Protestant, now religiously mixed canton
Neuchâtel	Neuchâtel	94	French-speaking, formerly Protestant, now religiously mixed canton
Fribourg	Fribourg	69 French-speakers 51 German-speakers	Bilingual, Catholic canton with French majority
Valais	Sion	68 French-speakers	Bilingual, Catholic canton with French majority
Bern	Bern	48	Bilingual canton with German majority, primarily Protestant
	Biel/Bienne	22 German-speakers 50 French speakers	Bilingual city
Solothurn	Solothurn	40	German-speaking, primarily Catholic canton
Aargau	Aarau	47	German-speaking, religiously mixed canton
Zug	Cham	48	German-speaking, Catholic canton
Zurich	Zurich	43	German-speaking, formerly Protestant, now religiously mixed canton
Total		596	

[a]Total sample, including foreigners.

two bilingual analysts. A number of questionnaires were scored by both, in order to assure a high degree of consistency.

After all the questionnaires had been coded, and a frequency count of the answers tabulated, the responses were regrouped into more inclusive categories which appear in Tables 21 and 22. The percentages in these two tables represent the number who gave one or more responses in a particular category—i.e., 68 percent of the German Swiss answering the question "Why are you proud to be Swiss?" gave one or more political answers (Table 21). Tables A-2 and A-3 record the composite categories listed on Tables 21 and 22, as well as the individual responses of Swiss youth which make up these categories.

TABLE A-2. Reasons given for being proud to be Swiss, by composite category and individual responses

Political

Neutral, independent country.
Not involved in wars, do not attempt to make wars.
Democracy, especially where one can vote.
Well governed, stable government.
One is free, also has freedom of speech, thought, human rights respected.
Switzerland doesn't have a monarchy.

Landscape

Small country, well located geographically.
Pretty country, beautiful landscape.

Socioeconomic

There are small differences between rich and poor, small class differences.
Rich country, plenty of everything, no poverty, high standard of living.
Proud of Swiss banks.
Stability of Swiss franc, can go anywhere with it.
Welfare state, provides for the citizen.
Little or no unemployment.
Good opportunities for jobs.

Quality of life

Peaceful country, has internal tranquility.
Clean country.
Not polluted.
Orderly country.
Few strikes.
One lives well, good quality of life.

Swiss qualities

Are hard workers, careful workers, make quality products.
Like Switzerland because I was born here, it's my fatherland.
Swiss have common sense.
Swiss are sympathetic people.

Diversity

Have good relations between cantons, cultural groups, harmony.
Like diversity of languages, customs.

Relations with other countries

Switzerland plays a fairly large role in world affairs.
Seat of world organizations.

TABLE A-2 cont.

Swiss are well liked, the country is well respected.
Switzerland helps developing countries.
Trustworthy country.
People like to come to Switzerland, tourists, refugees.

Not proud to be Swiss

Do not care if I am Swiss.
Not particularly proud to be Swiss.

Other reasons

Have good army, can go in the army.
Doesn't have many natural disasters.
Proud of Swiss history and ancestors who fought for freedom.
Adolescent answers (has good skiiers, etc.).
Adapts to times and conditions.
Land not overcrowded, not too much industry.
Highly industrialized, modern.

TABLE A-3. Reasons given for not being proud to be Swiss, by composite category and individual responses

Mentality, restrictive

Stagnant.
Too conservative.
Too restrictive.
People cold, petty, egoistic, chauvinistic, otherwise dislike mentality.
Too much censorship.
Swiss don't have much contact among themselves.
Swiss intolerant.

Politics

Too much politics.
Political lethargy, slow decision-making, poorly governed.
Against neutrality, nonalignment.

Elitism, influence

Too much influence of rich or aristocratic families or big companies.
Difference between rich and poor, class differences.

Against diversity

Don't like diversity of religion, customs.
Don't like diversity of language.
Dislike on part of other language group.
Dislike mentality of other language group.
Lack of cooperation between different cantons and language groups.

Foreign workers

Dislike fact that Swiss hostile toward foreign workers.
Don't like foreigners/foreign workers.

TABLE A-3 cont.

Overindustrialized

Too much industry, large buildings, large cities.
Overpopulated.
Too polluted.

Socioeconomic

Materialistic, capitalistic.
High cost of living.
High taxes.
Too much unemployment.
Lack of equality (e.g., for women, young people).
Swiss franc too high.

School

Too much school, otherwise don't like school.
Difference in school systems.

Nothing disliked

Nothing that I basically dislike.

Geography

Geography/weather (doesn't lie on ocean, too cold, too rainy).
No natural resources.
Small country, poorly located geographically.

Other reasons

Give too much money to developing countries.
Swiss don't like to give developing aid.
Switzerland too weak, plays too small a role in world affairs.
Swiss not respected abraod.
Rat race.
Adolescent answers (not enough for young people to do, speed limit too low
  for mopeds).
Too much prosperity, Swiss too soft.
Shady dealings, bank secrets.

Appendix II
German and French Questionnaires

F R A G E B O G E N

Liebe Schülerin, lieber Schüler,

Ich bitte Dich, mir bei einer Umfrage an verschiedenen Schweizer
Schulen zu helfen. Ich will Dir eine Reihe von Fragen stellen.
Bitte beantworte sie genau so, wie Du es für richtig hältst.
Fürchte Dich nicht vor falschen Antworten, denn oft gibt es
kein Falsch und kein Richtig, wo es sich um Deine Gefühle handelt.
Es gibt ja auch keine Noten dafür wie bei einer Probearbeit.
Wenn Du da oder dort keine Antwort geben kannst, dann lässt Du
die entsprechende Linie einfach leer.
　　　　　　*******
(Bitte bezeichne die richtige/entsprechende Antwort jeweils mit
einem X)

1) Wie ähnlich, glaubst Du, sind die folgenden Gruppen?

	sehr ähn-lich	ziemlich ähnlich	ich weiss nicht	ziemlich verschie-den	sehr ver-schieden
Tessiner + Italiener	☐	☐	☐	☐	☐
Tessiner + Welsche	☐	☐	☐	☐	☐
Tessiner + Deutschschweizer	☐	☐	☐	☐	☐
Deutschschweizer + Deutsche	☐	☐	☐	☐	☐
Deutschschweizer + Welsche	☐	☐	☐	☐	☐
Welschschweizer + Franzosen	☐	☐	☐	☐	☐
Welschschweizer + Deutsche	☐	☐	☐	☐	☐
Deutschschweizer + Franzosen	☐	☐	☐	☐	☐

2) Wie wichtig ist es für Dich, ein Bürger Deines Kantons zu sein?

- [ ] sehr wichtig
- [ ] ziemlich wichtig
- [ ] wenig wichtig
- [ ] überhaupt nicht wichtig

3) Wie wichtig ist es für Dich, ein Deutschschweizer zu sein?

- [ ] sehr wichtig
- [ ] ziemlich wichtig
- [ ] wenig wichtig
- [ ] überhaupt nicht wichtig

4) Wie wichtig ist Deine Religion für Dich?

- [ ] sehr wichtig
- [ ] ziemlich wichtig
- [ ] wenig wichtig
- [ ] überhaupt nicht wichtig

5) Wie wichtig ist es für Dich, ein Schweizerbürger zu sein?

- [ ] sehr wichtig
- [ ] ziemlich wichtig
- [ ] wenig wichtig
- [ ] überhaupt nicht wichtig

6) Stell Dir vor, dass eine grosse Umfrage über die Zukunft der Schweiz stattfindet. Glaubst Du, dass sich die Schweizer in den meisten Fragen einig wären?

- [ ] in praktisch allen Fragen einig
- [ ] in den meisten Fragen einig
- [ ] in der Hälfte der Fragen einig
- [ ] in den meisten Fragen uneinig
- [ ] in praktisch allen Fragen uneinig
- [ ] ich bin nicht sicher

7) Glaubst Du, dass Katholiken und Protestanten sich über die Zukunft der Schweiz einig wären?

- [ ] in praktisch allen Fragen einig
- [ ] in den meisten Fragen einig
- [ ] in der Hälfte der Fragen einig
- [ ] in den meisten Fragen uneinig
- [ ] in praktisch allen Fragen uneinig
- [ ] ich bin nicht sicher

8) Glaubst Du, dass deutschsprachige und französischsprachige Schweizer sich über die Zukunft der Schweiz einig wären?

- [ ] in praktisch allen Fragen einig
- [ ] in den meisten Fragen einig
- [ ] in der Hälfte der Fragen einig
- [ ] in den meisten Fragen uneinig
- [ ] in praktisch allen Fragen uneinig
- [ ] ich bin nicht sicher

9) Glaubst Du, dass sich Schweizer und Gastarbeiter über die Zukunft der Schweiz einig wären?

☐ in praktisch allen Fragen einig

☐ in den meisten Fragen einig

☐ in der Hälfte der Fragen einig

☐ in den meisten Fragen uneinig

☐ in praktisch allen Fragen uneinig

☐ ich bin nicht sicher

10) Glaubst Du, dass sich reiche und arme Leute über die Zukunft der Schweiz einig wären?

☐ in praktisch allen Fragen einig

☐ in den meisten Fragen einig

☐ in der Hälfte der Fragen einig

☐ in den meisten Fragen uneinig

☐ in praktisch allen Fragen uneinig

☐ ich bin nicht sicher

11) Glaubst Du, dass sich Leute aus grossen Städten und Leute vom Lande über die Zukunft der Schweiz einig wären?

☐ in praktisch allen Fragen einig

☐ in den meisten Fragen einig

☐ in der Hälfte der Fragen einig

☐ in den meisten Fragen uneinig

☐ in praktisch allen Fragen uneinig

☐ ich bin nicht sicher

12) Welches Land würdest Du als besten "Freund" der Schweiz bezeichnen?

bester Freund   ....

zweitbester Freund ....

drittbester Freund ....

13) Welche Regierung, glaubst Du, tut am meisten für die Bürger?

☐ Gemeinderegierung

☐ Kantonsregierung

☐ Bundesregierung

☐ ich bin nicht sicher

14) Welche Regierung, glaubst Du, tut am wenigsten für die Bürger?

☐ Gemeinderegierung

☐ Kantonsregierung

☐ Bundesregierung

☐ ich bin nicht sicher

15) In welchem dieser europäischen Länder würdest Du am liebsten
wohnen?

☐ Deutschland
☐ Frankreich
☐ Italien
☐ Oesterreich
☐ Holland
☐ Spanien

16) In welchen Ländern möchtest Du wohnen, wenn Du nicht in der
Schweiz wohnen könntest?

am liebsten ....

am zweitliebsten ....

zm drittliebsten ....

17) In welchen Kantonen möchtest Du in Zukunft einmal wohnen?
(bitte kreuze die entsprechenden Kantone an)

AG	AR	AI	BE	BL	BS	FR	GE	GL	GR	LU	NE

NW	OW	SG	SH	SO	SZ	TG	TI	UR	VD	VS	ZG	ZH

18) In welchen Kantonen möchtest Du bestimmt nie wohnen?
(bitte kreuze die entsprechenden Kantone an)

AG	AR	AI	BE	BL	BS	FR	GE	GL	GR	LE	NE

NW	OW	SG	SH	SO	SZ	TG	TI	UR	VD	VS	ZG	ZH

19) Welche Fremdsprache glaubst Du, ist für Dich später am
wichtigsten?

am wichtigsten ....

am zweitwichtigsten ....

20) Wieviele Prozente der Schweizer, denkst Du, sind

deutscher Muttersprache? ....

französischer Muttersprache? ....

italienischer Muttersprache? ....

21) Wie würdest Du die Beziehungen zwischen der deutschsprachigen
und der italienischsprachigen Schweiz beurteilen?

☐ sehr gut
☐ gut
☐ recht
☐ ziemlich schlecht
☐ schlecht
☐ ich bin nicht sicher

22) Wie würdest Du die Beziehungen zwischen der deutschsprachigen und französischsprachigen Schweiz beurteilen?

☐ sehr gut
☐ gut
☐ recht
☐ ziemlich schlecht
☐ schlecht
☐ ich bin nicht sicher

23) Wie würdest Du die Beziehungen zwischen Deutschschweizern und Gastarbeitern beurteilen?

☐ sehr gut
☐ gut
☐ recht
☐ ziemlich schlecht
☐ schlecht
☐ ich bin nicht sicher

24) Wie würdest Du die Beziehungen zwischen Deutschschweizern und Deutschen heurteilen?

☐ sehr gut
☐ gut
☐ recht
☐ ziemlich schlecht
☐ schlecht
☐ ich bin nicht sicher

25) In welcher Hinsicht, glaubst Du, könnten Dir gute Französisch-kenntnisse nützlich sein, sei es jetzt oder in Zukunft?

	wäre nützlich	wäre nicht nützlich
zur Unterhaltung mit Freunden	☐	☐
um neue Freunde zu gewinnen	☐	☐
beim Ausgehen mit Freund oder Freundin	☐	☐
für bessere Noten in der Schule	☐	☐
um eine Stelle zu finden	☐	☐
um in meinem zukünftigen Beruf vorwärts zu kommen	☐	☐
beim Reisen in andere Teile der Schweiz	☐	☐
beim Lesen, Fernsehen oder im Kino	☐	☐

26) Wie wichtig, glaubst Du, sind die folgenden Dinge für junge
Leute in der Schweiz zum Vorwärtskommen?

	äusserst wichtig	hilfreich	unwichtig
gute Noten in der Schule	☐	☐	☐
Beziehungen zu einfluss-reichen Leuten	☐	☐	☐
aus angesehener Familie stammend	☐	☐	☐
Universitätsausbildung	☐	☐	☐
aus der richtigen reli-giösen Gruppe stammend	☐	☐	☐
in der Schweiz geboren zu sein	☐	☐	☐
sowohl französisch als deutsch zu sprechen	☐	☐	☐
guter Charakter und um-gängliches Wesen	☐	☐	☐
harte Arbeit	☐	☐	☐
reiche Eltern	☐	☐	☐

27) Nenne die Namen von drei Personen aus der Geschichte der
Schweiz, die Du besonders bewunderst. Erkläre bitte in einem
oder zwei kurzen Sätzen, warum Du diese Personen gewählt hast.

....

....

....

....

******

....

....

....

....

******

....

....

....

....

******

28) Welche Schlachten hältst Du für die wichtigsten Schlachten der
Geschichte der Schweiz?

....

29) Beschreibe bitte in zwei oder drei Sätzen, warum Du froh bist,
Schweizer zu sein.

....

....

....

....

....

....

....

30) Was gefällt Dir auf der andern Seite an der Schweiz weniger gut?

....

....

....

....

....

....

....

31) Geschlecht

☐ männlich

☐ weiblich

32) Welche Sprache wird bei Dir zuhause gesprochen?

☐ deutsch

☐ französisch

☐ italienisch

☐ andere (welche?)   ....

☐ zweisprachig (welche?)............... + ...

33) In welchem Schuljahr bist Du?

☐ sechstes

☐ siebtes

☐ achtes

☐ neuntes

34) Wie alt bist Du?

....

35) Welche Ausbildung hat Dein Vater?
- ☐ Universität
- ☐ Mittelschule, Seminar
- ☐ Berufslehre
- ☐ keine Ausbildung

36) Welche Stellung hat Dein Vater?

....

37) Welche Ausbildung hat Deine Mutter?
- ☐ Universität
- ☐ Mittelschule, Seminar
- ☐ Berufslehre
- ☐ keine Ausbildung

38) Welcher Konfession gehörst Du an?
- ☐ katholisch
- ☐ protestantisch
- ☐ andere (welche?) ....

39) Bitte kreuze den Kanton an, in dem Du wohnst.

AG	AR	AI	BE	BL	BS	FR	GE	GL	GR	LU	NE

NW	OW	SG	SH	SO	SZ	TG	TI	UR	VD	VS	ZG	ZH

40) In welchen anderen Kantonen hast Du schon gewohnt?

AG	AR	AI	BE	BL	BS	FR	GE	GL	GR	LU	NE

NW	OW	SG	SH	SO	SZ	TG	TI	UR	VD	VS	ZG	ZH

41) In welchem Kanton hast Du am längsten gelebt?

AG	AR	AI	BE	BL	BS	FR	GE	GL	GR	LU	NE

NW	OW	SG	SH	SO	SZ	TG	TI	UR	VD	VS	ZG	ZH

42) Wo wohnst Du?
- ☐ in einer grösseren Stadt (Zürich, Basel, Genf, Bern, Lausanne, Winterthur, Luzern)
- ☐ in einem Vorort einer dieser Städte
- ☐ in einer anderen, kleineren Stadt
- ☐ in einer Ortschaft auf dem Land

43) Welche Schule besuchst Du?
- ☐ Gymnasium
- ☐ Sekundarschule

44) Bist Du schon für eine Zeitspanne von mehr als zwei Wochen in der welschen Schweiz gewesen?
- ☐ ja
- ☐ nein

45) Hast Du Verwandte oder Bekannte in der welschen Schweiz?

☐ ja

☐ nein

46) Welcher Nationlität bist Du?

☐ Schweizer

☐ Italiener

☐ Franzose

☐ Deutscher

☐ andere (welche?) ....

Q U E S T I O N N A I R E

Introduction

Nous sommes en train de faire une enquête dans plusieurs écoles
pour savoir ce que les jeunes de votre âge pensent. Nous allons
vous poser quelques questions, essayez d'y répondre exactement
comme vous pensez. Ne croyez pas qu'il y ait une réponse vraie
et une réponse fausse à chaque question, car toute les réponses
sont également valables. Voici comment je vais vous poser ces
questions: je vais vous lire à haute voix les questions que
vous voyez devant vous et vous allez répondre, soit en écrivant
ce que vous pensez, soit en mettant une croix dans la case qui
correspond à ce que vous voulez répondre. Il se peut que vous
ne sachiez pas la réponse, alors vous pouvez le dire aussi en
mettant une croix dans la case "je ne sais pas" ou en n'écrivant
rien du tout.

****

1) Quelles sont à votre avis les affinités entre les groupes
   suivants?

	très semblables	assez semblables	je ne sais pas	assez différents	très différents
Tessinois + Italiens	☐	☐	☐	☐	☐
Tessinois + Suisses romands	☐	☐	☐	☐	☐
Tessinois + Suisses allemands	☐	☐	☐	☐	☐
Suisses allemands + Allemands	☐	☐	☐	☐	☐
Suisses allemands + Suisses romands	☐	☐	☐	☐	☐
Suisses romands + Français	☐	☐	☐	☐	☐
Suisses romands + Allemands	☐	☐	☐	☐	☐
Suisses allemands + Français	☐	☐	☐	☐	☐

2) Etre citoyen de ton canton, est-ce pour toi

☐ très important
☐ assez important
☐ peu important
☐ sans aucune importance

3) Etre Suisse romand, est-ce pour toi

☐ très important
☐ assez important
☐ peu important
☐ sanc aucune importance

4) Quelle importance attaches-tu à la religion?

☐ très important
☐ assez important
☐ peu important
☐ sans aucune importance

5) Etre un citoyen suisse, est-ce pour toi

☐ très important
☐ assez important
☐ peu important
☐ sans aucune importance

6) Suppose que les Suisses votent sur plusieurs points importants touchant à l'avenir du pays. Crois-tu que les Suisses seraient

☐ d'accord sur pratiquement tous les points
☐ d'accord sur la plupart des points
☐ d'accord sur la moitié
☐ pas d'accord sur la plupart des points
☐ pas d'accord sur quasiment tous les points
☐ je ne suis pas sûr

7) Crois-tu que les Catholiques et les Protestants seraient

☐ d'accord sur pratiquement tous les points
☐ d'accord sur la plupart des points
☐ d'accord sur la moitié
☐ pas d'accord sur la plupart des points
☐ pas d'accord sur quasiment tous les points
☐ je ne suis pas sûr

8) Crois-tu que les Romands et les Alémaniques seraient

☐ d'accord sur pratiquement tous les points
☐ d'accord sur la plupart des points
☐ d'accord sur la moitié
☐ pas d'accord sur la plupart des points
☐ pas d'accord sur quasiment tous les points
☐ je ne suis pas sûr

9) Crois-tu que les Suisses et les travailleurs étrangers seraient

☐ d'accord sur pratiquement tous les points
☐ d'accord sur la plupart des points
☐ d'accord sur la moitié
☐ pas d'accord sur la plupart des points
☐ pas d'accord sur quasiment tous les points
☐ je ne suis pas sûr

10) Crois-tu que les gens riches et les gens pauvres seraient
- ☐ d'accord sur pratiquement tous les points
- ☐ d'accord sur la plupart des points
- ☐ d'accord sur la moitié
- ☐ pas d'accord sur la plupart des points
- ☐ pas d'accord sur quasiment tous les points
- ☐ je ne suis pas sûr

11) Crois-tu que les citadins et les campagnards seraient
- ☐ d'accord sur pratiquement tous les points
- ☐ d'accord sur la plupart des points
- ☐ d'accord sur la moitié
- ☐ pas d'accord sur la plupart des points
- ☐ pas d'accord sur quasiment tous les points
- ☐ je ne suis pas sûr

12) Quels sont à votre avis les trois pays les plus amis de la Suisse? (Cite en trois, par ordre d'importance decroissant)

meilleur ami ....

second ....

troisième ....

13) A ton avis, quelle autorité fait le plus pour le bien des citoyens?
- ☐ le gouvernement communal
- ☐ le gouvernement cantonal
- ☐ le gouvernement fédéral
- ☐ je ne suis pas sûr

14) Et quelle autorité fait le moins pour le bien des citoyens?
- ☐ le gouvernement communal
- ☐ le gouvernement cantonal
- ☐ le gouvernement fédéral
- ☐ je ne suis pas sûr

15) Lequel des pays européens suivants choisirais-tu comme domicile?
- ☐ l'Allemagne
- ☐ la France
- ☐ l'Italie
- ☐ l'Autriche
- ☐ les Pays-Bas
- ☐ l'Espagne

16) Dans quels pays aimerais-tu vivre si tu ne pouvais pas vivre en Suisse?

premier choix ....

deuxième choix ....

troisième choix ....

17) Dans quels cantons aimerais-tu vivre une fois? (mets une croix dans la case qui correspond a ce que tu veux répondre)

AG	AR	AI	BE	BL	BS	FR	GE	GL	GR	LU	NE

NW	OW	SG	SH	SO	SZ	TG	TI	UR	VD	VS	ZG	ZH

18) Dans quels cantons n'aimerais-tu définitivement jamais vivre?

AG	AR	AI	BE	BL	BS	FR	GE	GL	GR	LU	NE

NW	OW	SG	SH	SO	SZ	TG	TI	UR	VD	VS	ZG	ZH

19) Quelles langues étrangères crois-tu sont les plus importantes pour ton future?

la première   ....

la seconde   ....

20) Combien de pourcents des Suisses, crois-tu, parlent l'allemand

comme première langue? ....

le francais comme pre-
mière langue?   ....

l'italien comme pre-
mière langue?   ....

21) Comment qualifierais-tu les relations entre les Suisses romands et les Suisses italiens?

☐ très bonnes
☐ bonnes
☐ passables
☐ mauvaises
☐ très mauvaises
☐ je ne suis pas sûr

22) Comment qualifierais-tu les relations entre les Suisses romands et les Suisses allemands?

☐ très bonnes
☐ bonnes
☐ passables
☐ mauvaises
☐ très mauvaises
☐ je ne suis pas sûr

23) Comment qualifierais-tu les relations entre Suisses romands et travailleurs étrangers?

☐ très bonnes
☐ bonnes
☐ passables
☐ mauvaises
☐ très mauvaises
☐ je ne suis pas sûr

24) Comment qualifierais-tu les relations entre Suisses romands et Français?

- [ ] très bonnes
- [ ] bonnes
- [ ] passables
- [ ] mauvaises
- [ ] très mauvaises
- [ ] je ne suis pas sûr

25) A quels points de vue, penses-tu, une bonne connaissance de la langue allemande te serait utile (maintenant ou à l'avenir)? (Mets une croix pour chaque partie de la question)

	utile	inutile
pour discuter avec des amis	[ ]	[ ]
pour te faire de nouveaux amis	[ ]	[ ]
pour sortir avec une fille/un garçon	[ ]	[ ]
pour avoir de meilleures notes à l'école	[ ]	[ ]
pour trouver du travail	[ ]	[ ]
pour progresser dans le domaine où j'espère travailler	[ ]	[ ]
pour voyager en Suisse allemande	[ ]	[ ]
pour la lecture, la TV ou le cinéma	[ ]	[ ]

26) Que faut-il, à ton avis, pour qu'on réussisse en Suisse? (entoure une réponse: mets une croix pour chaque partie de la question)

	très important	assez important	sans importance
avoir de bonnes notes à l'école	[ ]	[ ]	[ ]
connaître les gens qu'il faut	[ ]	[ ]	[ ]
appartenir à une bonne famille	[ ]	[ ]	[ ]
avoir une formation universitaire	[ ]	[ ]	[ ]
être de la confession qu'il faut	[ ]	[ ]	[ ]
être né en Suisse	[ ]	[ ]	[ ]
parler le français et l'allemand	[ ]	[ ]	[ ]
avoir un bon caractère	[ ]	[ ]	[ ]
travailler dur	[ ]	[ ]	[ ]
avoir des parents riches	[ ]	[ ]	[ ]

27) Cite trois personnes de l'histoire suisse que tu admires tout
particulièrement et dis pourquoi (en deux ou trois phrases).

....

....

....

....

****

....

....

....

....

****

....

....

....

....

28) Quelles sont les batailles de l'histoire suisse qui te
paraissent les plus importantes?

....

29) Dis en deux ou trois phrases pourquoi tu es fier/fière d'etre
suisse.

....

....

....

....

....

....

....

30) De l'autre côté, qu'est-ce qui te déplaît en Suisse?

....

....

....

....

....

....

....

31) Sexe

☐ garçon
☐ fille

32) Quelle langue parles tu a la maison?

☐ l'allemand
☐ le français
☐ l'italien
☐ une autre (laquelle?)..............................
☐ bilingue .... +.............

33) En quelle année scolaire es-tu?

☐ sixième
☐ septième
☐ huitième
☐ neuvième

34) Quel âge as-tu?

....

35) Quelle est la formation de ton père?

☐ formation universitaire
☐ formation collegienne
☐ apprentissage
☐ pas d'apprentissage

36) Quelle est sa position présente?

....

37) Quelle est la formation de ta mère?

☐ formation universitaire
☐ formation collégienne
☐ apprentissage
☐ pas d'apprentissage

38) Quelle est ta confession?

☐ catholique
☐ protestante
☐ autre (laquelle?) ....

39) Dans quel canton habites-tu?

AG	AR	AI	BE	BL	BS	FR	GE	GL	GR	LU	NE	
NW	OW	SG	SH	SO	SZ	TG	TI	UR	VD	VS	ZG	ZH

40) Dans quels cantons as-tu déjà habité?

AG	AR	AI	BE	BL	BS	FR	GE	GL	GR	LU	NE	
NW	OW	SG	SH	SO	SZ	TG	TI	UR	VD	VS	ZG	ZH

41) Dans quel canton as-tu vécu le plus longtemps?

AG	AR	AI	BE	BL	BS	FR	GE	GL	GR	LU	NE

NW	OW	SG	SH	SO	SZ	TG	TI	UR	VD	VS	ZG	ZH

42) Où habites-tu?

☐ dans une grande ville (Zurich, Bâle, Genève, Berne, Lausanne, Winterthour ou Lucerne)

☐ dans la banlieue d'une de ces villes

☐ dans une autre ville (plus petite)

☐ dans un village (à la campagne)

43) Type de ton école?

☐ Gymnase

☐ Ecole secondaires

44) As-tu déjà été en Suisse allemande pour la durée de plus de deux semaines?

☐ oui

☐ non

45) As-tu de la parenté ou des connaissances dans la Suisse allemande?

☐ oui

☐ non

46) De quelle nationalité es-tu?

☐ Suisse

☐ Italienne

☐ Française

☐ Allemande

☐ autre (laquelle?) ....

Bibliography

Allemann, Fritz René
    1968   *25 mal die Schweiz*. Munich: R. Piper.
Almond, Gabriel
    1946   "Comparative Political Systems." *Journal of Politics* 18:391-409.
Almond, Gabriel, and Sidney Verba
    1963   *The Civic Culture*. Princeton, N.J.: Princeton University Press.
Altermatt, Urs, and Hans Utz
    1976   "Hitler Bild und Personalisierungs—Problem, Vergleichende
          Analyse von Schulgeschichtsbüchern der Schweiz." *Zeit-*
          geschichte 4:25-38.
Andermatt, Urs
    1972   *Der Weg der Schweizer Katholiken ins Ghetto*. Zurich: Benziger.
Annuaire Statistique de la Suisse
    1976, 1977, 1979   Basel: Birkhäuser.
Auerbach, F.E.
    1965   *The Power of Prejudice in South African Education*. Capetown: A.A.
          Balkema.
Bassand, Michel
    1975   "The Jura Problem." *Journal of Peace Research* 12:139-150.
Béguelin, Roland
    1973   *Un faux témoin, la Suisse*. Lausanne: Edition du Monde.
Bellah, Robert
    1967   "Civil Religion in America." *Daedalus* 96:1-21.
Berelson, Bernard
    1952   *Content Analysis*. Glencoe, Ill.: Free Press.
Bericht des Bundesrates an die Bundesversammlung über das zweite Volksbegehren gegen
    Ueberfremdung
    1969   Bern.
Bericht über die pädogogischen Rekrutenprüfungen im Jahre 1968
    1969   Bern.
Bessire, P.O.
    1935   *Histoire du Jura et de l'ancien evêché de Bâle*. Porrentruy.
Bickel, Wilhelm
    1947   *Bevölkerungsgeschichte und Bevölkerungspolitik der Schweiz seit dem Aus-*
          gang des Mittelalters. Zürich: Büchergilde Gutenberg.

184 | Bibliography

Bierstedt, Robert
    1955 "The Writers of Textbooks." In Lee J. Cronbach, ed., *Text Materials in Modern Education*. Urbana: University of Illinois Press.
Bohnenblust, Ernst
    1974 *Geschichte der Schweiz*. Erlenbach-Zürich: Eugen Rentsch.
Boltanski, Luc
    1967 *Le bonheur suisse*. Paris: Editions de Minuit.
Bonjour, Edgar
    1938 In Hans Nabholz, Leonard von Muralt, Richard Feller, and Edgar Bonjour, *Geschichte der Schweiz*, vol. 2. Zürich: Schulthess.
    1952 *A Short History of Switzerland*. Oxford: Clarendon Press.
Braun, Rudolf
    1970 *Sozio-kulturelle Probleme der Eingliederung italienischer Arbeitskräfte in der Schweiz*. Erlenbach-Zürich: Eugen Rentsch.
Brooks, Robert C.
    1930 *Civic Training in Switzerland*. Chicago: University of Chicago Press.
Bryce, James
    1921 *Modern Democracies*, vol. 1. London: Macmillan.
Cartwright, D.P.
    1953 "Analysis of Qualitative Material." In Leon Festinger and David Katz, eds., *Research Methods in the Behavioral Sciences*. New York: Holt, Rinehart and Winston.
Casaulta, Giachen Guisep
    1966 "Graubünden auch sprachlich eine Schweiz im Kleinen." *Civitas* 22:65-68.
Castells, Manuel
    1975 "Immigrant Workers and Class Struggles in Advanced Capitalism: The Western European Experience." *Politics and Society* 5:33-66.
Castles, Stephen, and Godula Kosack
    1973 *Immigrant Workers and the Class Structure*. London: Oxford University Press.
Cicourel, Aaron V.
    1964 *Methods and Measurement in Sociology*. New York: Free Press.
Codding, George Arthur
    1961 *The Federal Government of Switzerland*. Boston: Houghton Mifflin.
Daalder, Hans
    1974a "On Building Consociational Nations: The Cases of the Netherlands and Switzerland." In Kenneth McRae, ed., *Consociational Democracy*. The Carleton Library, no. 74. Toronto: McClelland and Stuart.
    1974b "The Consociational Democracy Theme." *World Politics* 26: 604-621.
Dawson, Richard E., and Kenneth Prewitt
    1969 *Political Socialization*. Boston: Little, Brown.
Deutsch, Karl
    1976 *Die Schweiz als ein paradigmatischer Fall politischer Integration*. Bern: Verlag Haupt.

Dubs, R.
1970 "Der Staatspolitische Aspekt." Lecture in the series "Die Schweiz und die Ausländischen Arbeitskräfte," Instituts für Betriebswirtschaft, Hochschule St. Gallen, March 12-13.

Dunn, James
1971 "Social Cleavage, Party Systems, and Political Integration: A Comparison of the Belgian and Swiss Experiences." Ph.D. dissertation, University of Pennsylvania. Ann Arbor, Mich.: University Microfilms.
1972 "Consociational Democracy and Language Conflict: A Comparison of the Belgian and Swiss Experiences." *Comparative Political Studies* 5:3-39.

Durkheim, Emile
1961 *Moral Education.* New York: Free Press.

Egger, Eugene, and Emile Blanc
1974 *Education in Switzerland.* Geneva: Swiss Educational Documentation Center.

Engeli, Arne
1972 *Politische Bildung in der Schweiz.* Frauenfeld and Stuttgart: Verlag Huber.

Enloe, Cynthia
1973 *Conflict and Political Development.* Boston: Little, Brown.

Ernst, Fritz
1954 *Der Helvetismus, Einheit in der Vielheit.* Zürich: Fretz und Wasmuth Verlag.

Etzioni, Amitai
1965 *Political Unification: A Comparative Study of Leaders and Forces.* New York: Holt, Rinehart and Winston.

Falke, Konrad
1915 *Das demokratische Ideal und unsere nationale Erziehung.* Zürich: Rascher.

Fasel, Bruno
1959 "Die deutsche Minderheit in Kanton Freiburg." *Die Schweiz.* Bern: Buri.

Fick, Fritz
1910 *Gibt es eine schweizerische Nation und Kultur?* Zürich and Leipzig: Verlag Rascher.

Fischer, Hardi, and Uri P. Trier
1962 *Das Verhältnis zwischen Deutschschweizer und Westschweizer: Eine sozialpsychologische Untersuchung.* Bern: Verlag Huber.

Fondation pour la collaboration Confédérale
1973 *Le fédéralisme réexaminé,* vol. 1. Zürich: Benziger.

Gasser, Adolf
1965 *Der Jura in Kanton Bern, 1815-1965.* Bern: Staatskanzlei.

Girod, Roger
1975 "Les travailleurs étrangers en Suisse: ouverture et domination." *L'année sociologue* 26:21-41.

Glass, Harold
1975 "Subcultural Segmentation and Consensual Politics: The

Swiss Experience." Ph.D. dissertation, University of North Carolina.

Glassner, Barry, and Jay Couzine
1979 "Library Research as Fieldwork: A Strategy for Qualitative Content Analysis." Paper presented at annual meeting of the American Sociological Association, Boston, August.

Glazer, Nathan, and Daniel P. Moynihan
1970 *Beyond the Melting Pot.* Cambridge, Mass.: Massachusetts Institute of Technology Press.

Greyerz, Walo von
1959 "Die Schwäche der Starken." In *Die Kraft der Schwachen in der Eidgenossenschaft*, Yearbook of the New Helvetic Society.

Grichting, E.
1959 "Die deutsche Minderheit im Wallis." *Die Schweiz*. Bern: Buri.

Hadorn, Werner, Stefan Kaspar, Peter L. Rothenbühler, and Stefan Thomi
1971 "Mehrsprachige Schweiz: Kaum Einheit in der Vielfalt." *Sonntags Journal* 3 (June):14-22.

Halliday, Fred
1979 "The Arc of Revolutions: Iran, Afghanistan, South Yemen, Ethiopia." *Race and Class* 20 (Spring):373-390.

Hamilton, Alexander, James Madison, and John Jay
1941 [1788] *The Federalist.* New York: Modern Library.

Hamilton, Charles, and Stokely Carmichael
1967 *Black Power.* New York: Random House.

Harder, Hans-Joachim
1978 *Der Kanton Jura: Ursachen und Schritte zur Lösung eines Schweizer Minderheitenproblems.* Bern: Verlag Lang.

Hegnauer, Cyril
1947 *Das Sprachenrecht der Schweiz.* Zürich: Schultess.

Heiman, G.
1966 "The 19th-Century Legacy: Nationalism and Patriotism in Canada." In P. Russell, ed., *Nationalism in Canada.* Toronto: McGraw-Hill.

Heisler, Martin O., ed.
1977 "Ethnic Conflict in the World Today: An Introduction." *Annals of the American Academy of Political and Social Science* 433:1-5.

Henecka, Hans Peter
1972 *Die jurassischen Separatisten: Eine Studie zur Soziologie des ethnischen Konflikts und der sozialen Bewegung.* Meisenheim am Glan: Verlag Anton Hain.

Herberg, Will
1955 *Protestant-Catholic-Jew.* New York: Doubleday.

Hewitt, Christopher
1977 "Majorities and Minorities: A Comparative Survey of Ethnic Violence." *Annals of the American Academy of Political and Social Science* 433:150-160.

Hodgetts, A.B.
 1968 *What Culture? What Heritage? A Study of Civic Education in Canada.*
      Curriculum Series 5. Toronto: Ontario Institute for Studies
      in Education.
Hoffmann-Nowotny, Hans Joachim
 1973 *Soziologie des Fremdarbeiterproblems: Eine theoretische und empirische*
      Analyse am Beispiel der Schweiz. Stuttgart: Enke Verlag.
 1974 "Immigrant minorities in Switzerland: Sociological, legal, and
      political aspects." *Current Research in Sociology*, 8th World Con-
      gress of Sociology, The Hague.
Huber, Hans
 1946 *How Switzerland Is Governed.* Zurich: Schweizer Spiegel Verlag.
Hughes, Christopher
 1962 *The Parliament of Switzerland.* London: Cassell.
 1975 *Switzerland.* London: Ernest Benn.
Imboden, Max
 1964 *Helvetisches Malaise.* Zürich: EVZ Verlag.
Jaffa, Harry V.
 1959 *Crisis of the House Divided.* New York: Doubleday.
Johnstone, John C.
 1969 *Young People's Images of Canadian Society.* Studies of the Canadian
      Royal Commission on Bilingualism and Biculturalism. Ottawa:
      Information Canada.
Joos, H.
 1974 "Sprechverhalten in Mundart und Hochsprache, ein Vergleich
      zwischen 7-jährigen Kindern und Erwachsenen." Ph.D. dis-
      sertation, University of Bern.
Kägi, Werner
 1959 "Demokratie und Minderheit." *Die Schweiz.* Bern: Buri.
Keech, W.R.
 1972 "Linguistic Diversity and Political Conflict: Some Observa-
      tions Based on Four Swiss Cantons." *Comparative Politics*
      4:387-404.
Kerr, Henry, Jr.
 1974 *Switzerland: Social Cleavages and Partisan Conflict.* Sage Professional
      Papers in Contemporary Political Sociology. Beverly Hills,
      Calif.: Sage.
 1975 "National Unity and Social Tranquility: Several Theories of
      Swiss 'Exceptionalism.'" Paper presented at IPSA Round-
      Table Discussion on National and Class Interests in Multi-
      Ethnic Societies, Dubrovnik, September.
Kindleberger, Charles P.
 1967 *Europe's Postwar Growth.* Cambridge, Mass.: Harvard University
      Press.
Kohn, H.
 1956 *Nationalism and Liberty: The Swiss Example.* London: Allen and
      Unwin.

Kommission der 24
   1968   *Bericht zur Jurafrage.* Biel: Graphische Anstalt Schueler.
Kracauer, S.
   1952   "The Challenge of Qualitative Content Analysis." *Public Opinion Quarterly* 16 (Winter):631-642.
Lamy, Paul G.
   1975   "Political Socialization of French and English Canadian Youth." In Elia Zureik and Robert Pike, eds., *Socialization and Values in Canadian Society.* Toronto: McClelland and Stewart.
Lehmbruch, Gerhard
   1967   *Proporzdemokratie: Politisches System und politische Kultur im der Schweiz und Oesterreich.* Tübingen: Mohr.
   1968   "Konkordanzdemokratie im politischen System der Schweiz: Ein Literaturbericht." *Politische Vierteljahresschrift* 9:443-459.
Ley, Katharina
   1979   *Frauen in der Emigration.* Frauenfeld and Stuttgart: Verlag Huber.
Lijphart, Arend
   1968   "Typologies of Democratic Systems." *Comparative Political Studies* 1:3-44.
   1969   "Consociational Democracy." *World Politics* 21:207-225.
   1977a *Democracy in Plural Societies.* New Haven, Conn.: Yale University Press.
   1977b "Political Theories and the Explanation of Ethnic Conflict in the Western World: Falsified Predictions and Plausible Postdictions." In Milton J. Esman, ed., *Ethnic Conflict in the Western World.* Ithaca, N.Y.: Cornell University Press.
Lorwin, Val
   1974   "Segmented Pluralism: Ideological Cleavages and Political Cohesion in the Smaller European Democracies." In Kenneth McRae, ed., *Consociational Democracy.* The Carleton Library, no. 79. Toronto: McClelland and Stewart.
Lüthy, Herbert
   1962   "Has Switzerland a Future? The Dilemma of the Small Nation." *Encounter* 19:23-34.
   1969   *Die Schweiz als Antithese.* Zürich: Verlag der Arche.
McRae, Kenneth D.
   1964   *Switzerland: Example of Cultural Coexistence. Contemporary Affairs.* Toronto: Canadian Institute of Internal Affairs.
   1974   Introduction to Kenneth McRae, ed., *Consociational Democracy.* The Carleton Library, no. 79. Toronto: McClelland and Stewart.
   1975   "The Structure of Political Cleavages and Political Conflict: Reflections on the Swiss Case." Paper presented at ECP/CES Workshop on Contemporary Switzerland, Geneva, June.
   1978   "The Jura Question." (unpublished manuscript)
Marchi, Otto
   1975   "Wilhelm Tells geschichtliche Sendung." *Merian* (January): 18-20.

Mattmüller, Felix
  1975 *Grundlagen und Entwurf eines Gesetzes für Erziehung und Unterricht.*
       Basel: Z-Verlag.
Mayer, Kurt
  1951 "Cultural Pluralism and Linguistic Equilibrium in Switzer-
       land." *American Sociological Review* 16:157-163.
  1952 *The Population of Switzerland.* New York: Columbia University
       Press.
  1967 "Migration, Cultural Tensions, and Foreign Relations: Swit-
       zerland." *Journal of Conflict Resolution* 11:139-152.
  1968 "The Jura Problem: Ethnic Conflict in Switzerland." *Social Re-
       search* 35:707-741.
  1971 "Foreign Workers in Switzerland and Austria." *European Demo-
       graphic Bulletin* 2:93-101.
  1975 "Intra-European Migration During the Past Twenty Years."
       International Migration Review 9:441-447.
  1977 "Groupes linguistiques en Suisse." *Recherches sociologiques*
       8:74-94.
Melich, Anna
  1978 "Personnalité et socialisation pré-politique en Suisse." Ph.D.
       dissertation, University of Geneva.
Merriam, Charles E.
  1966 [1931] *The Making of Citizens.* New York: Teacher's College
       Press, Columbia University.
Meyer, Karl
  1952 "Die mehrsprachige Schweiz." *Mitteilungen der Antiquarischen
       Gesellschaft* 37:117-127.
Naroll, Raoul
  1964 "Some Problems for Research in Switzerland." In Viola E.
       Garfield and Ernestine Friedl, eds., *Symposium on Community
       Studies in Anthropology.* Seattle: American Ethnological Society.
Niemitz, Heinz
  1970 "Zur Schweizerischen Konkordanzdemokratie." *Schweizer
       Rundschau* 69:66-89.
Nordlinger, Eric A.
  1972 "Conflict Regulation in Divided Societies." *Occasional Papers in
       International Affairs* no. 29. Center for International Affairs,
       Harvard University.
Oberg, Kjell
  1974 "Treatment of Immigrant Workers in Sweden." *International
       Labour Review* 110:1-16.
Pedrazzini, Mario M.
  1952 *La lingua italiana nel diritto federale svizzero.* Locarno: Pedrazzini.
Peer, Andri
  1975 "Glanz und Elend einer Minderheit." *Merian* 28:76, 103-104.
Peer, Andri, and Jon Pult
  1974 *The Origins of Reto-Romansch.* Bern: Pro Helvetia Press Service.
Petersen, William
  1975 "On the Subnations of Western Europe." In Nathan Glazer

and Daniel P. Moynihan, eds., *Ethnicity: Theory and Experience.* Cambridge, Mass.: Harvard University Press.

Phillippe, Vincent
  1979 *Republik Jura, Der 23. Kanton der Schweiz.* Frauenfeld: Verlag Huber.

Piaget, Jean
  1951 "The Development of the Idea of a Homeland and of Relations with Other Countries." *International Social Science Bulletin* 3:561-571.

Pichard, Alain
  1975 *Vingt Suisses à decouvrir.* Lausanne: Editions 24 Heures.

Pool, Ithiel de Sola, ed.
  1959 *Trends in Content Analysis.* Urbana: University of Illinois Press.

Pratt, David
  1975 "The Role of School Textbooks in Canada." In Elia Zureik and Robert M. Pike, eds., *Socialization and Values in Canadian Society,* vol. 1. The Carleton Library, no. 84. Toronto: McClelland and Stewart.

Prongue, Bernard
  1973 *Histoire populaire du Jura de 1943 à 1973.* Porrentruy: Editions jurassiennes.

Rabuska, Allan, and Kenneth Shepsle
  1972 *Politics in Plural Societies: A Theory of Democratic Instability.* Columbus, Ohio: Merrill.

Reymond, F.L.
  1965 "La question jurassienne et l'évolution du mouvement séparatiste 1959-1964." *Annuaire de l'association suisse de science politique* 5:29-84.

Reynold, Gonzague de
  1968 *Destin du Jura.* Lausanne: Editions Rencontre.

Richert, Jean Pierre
  1974 "The Impact of Ethnicity on the Perception of Heroes and Historical Symbols." *Canadian Review of Sociology and Anthropology* 11:156-163.

Rickover, H.G.
  1962 *Swiss Schools and Ours: Why Theirs Are Better.* Boston: Little, Brown.

Rist, Ray C.
  1979 "Migration and Marginality: Guestworkers in Germany and France." *Daedalus* 108 (Spring):95-108.

Rocher, Guy
  1976 "History and Social Change: Some Myths and Realities." Alan B. Plaunt Memorial Lectures, delivered at Carleton University, Ottawa, May 6-8.

Rohr, Jean
  1972 *La Suisse Contemporaine.* Paris: Librairie Armand Colin.

Rougemont, Denis de
  1965   *La Suisse ou l'histoire d'un peuple heureux.* Lausanne: Librairie
         Hachette.
Rousseau, Jean-Jacques
  1953   [1772] "Considerations on the Government of Poland" in *Political Writings* (trans. Frederick Watkins). New York: Nelson.
Ruffieux, Roland
  1962   "Les incidences politiques du plurilinguisme" *Res Publica*
         4 (259-270).
Salis, Jean Rudolphe de
  1971   *La Suisse diverse et paradoxale.* Neuchâtel: La Baconnière.
Schäppi, Peter
  1971   *Der Schutz sprachlicher und konfessioneller Minderheiten im Recht von Bund und Kantonen.* Zürich: Polygraphischer Verlag.
Schwarzenbach, Rudolf
  1969   *Die Stellung der Mundart in der deutschsprachigen Schweiz.* Frauenfeld: Huber.
Schweizerische Bankgesellschaft
  1976   "Das Volkeinkommen der Kantone, 1970-1975." Zürich.
Schweizerische Konferenz der kantonalen Erziehungsdirektoren
  1976   "Empfehlungen und Beschlüsse betreffend Einführung, Reform und Koordination des Unterrichts in der zweiten Landessprache für alle Schüler während der obligatorischen Schulzeit." Geneva, Oct. 20, 1975.
Scope Institute for Market and Opinion Research
  1973   "Die Fremdsprachenkenntisse der Schweizer." Lucerne, January.
Sidjanski, Dusan
  1975   "Environment Politique en Suisse." In Dusan Sidjanski, Charles Roig, Henry Kerr, Ronald Inglehart, and Jacques Nicola, eds., *Les Suisses et la Politique.* Bern: Herbert Lang.
Siegenthaler, Jürg
  1975   "Current Problems of Trade Union-Party Relations in Switzerland: Reorientation Versus Inertia." *Industrial and Labour Relations Review* 28:264-281.
Siegfried, André
  1956   *La Suisse, démocratie témoin.* Neuchâtel: La Baconnière.
Simpson, George, and J. Milton Yinger
  1965   *Racial and Cultural Minorities.* New York: Harper and Row.
Soloveytchik, George
  1954   *Switzerland in Perspective.* London: Oxford University Press.
Steinberg, Jonathan
  1976   *Why Switzerland?* London: Cambridge University Press.
Steiner, Jürg
  1971   "The Principles of Majority and Proportionality." *British Journal of Political Science* 1:63-70.

1974   *Amicable Agreement Versus Majority Rule.* Chapel Hill: University of North Carolina Press.
Stöckli, Walter A.
    1970   *Church, State and School in Switzerland and the United States.* European University Papers. Bern: Herbert Lang.
Swiss National Commission for UNESCO
    1957   "Programmes et manuels d'histoire, suggestions en vue de leur amélioration." Rorschach: Lopfe-Benz.
Thompson, David
    1958   *Democracy in France.* London: Oxford University Press.
Tocqueville, Alexis de
    1969   [1850] *Democracy in America* (trans. George Lawrence). New York: Doubleday, Anchor Books.
Troxler, Ferdinand
    1975   "Two Burning Issues in Switzerland." *Free Labour World* 295: 13-14.
Trudel, Marcel, and Genevieve Jain
    1968   *Canadian History Textbooks: A Comparative Study.* Royal Commission on Bilingualism and Biculturalism, no. 5. Ottawa: Queen's Printer.
Van den Berghe, Pierre
    1971a "Ethnicity: The African Experience." *International Social Science Journal* 23:507-518.
    1971b "Pluralism and the Polity: A Theoretical Exploration." In Leo Kuper and M.G. Smith, eds., *Pluralism in Africa.* Berkeley and Los Angeles: University of California Press.
    1976   "Ethnic Pluralism in Industrial Societies: A Special Case?" *Ethnicity* 3:242-255.
Die Volkswirtschaft
    1970, 1975, 1978, 1979   43 (April 1970), 49 (February 1975), 52 (March 1978), 53 (March 1979).
Vollenweider, Alice
    1975   "Die hybride Provinz." *Merian* 28 (January): 70-74.
Warburton, T.
    1976   "Nationalism and Language in Switzerland and Canada." In A.D. Smith, ed., *Nationalist Movements.* London: Macmillan.
Weilenmann, Herman
    1925   *Die vielsprachige Schweiz: Eine Lösung des Nationalitätenproblems.* Basel: Am Rhein Verlag.
    1962   "La question linguistique en Suisse." *Res Publica* 4:225-237.
Werner, Heinz
    1977   "Some Current Topics of Labour Migration in Europe, Some Past Facts and Figures." *International Migration* 15:300-306.
Williams, Robin M.
    1977   *Mutual Accommodation, Ethnic Conflict, and Cooperation.* Minneapolis: University of Minnesota Press.
    1979   "Structure and Process in Ethnic Relations: Increased Knowl-

edge and Unanswered Questions." Paper presented at annual meeting of the American Sociological Association, Boston, August.

Williamson, Lloyd Paul
1969 "The Image of Indians, French Canadians, and Americans in Authorized Ontario High School Textbooks: 1890-1930." M.A. thesis, Institute of Canadian Studies, Carleton University, Ottawa.

Wirth, Louis
1945 In Ralph Linton, ed., *The Science of Man in World Crisis*. New York: Columbia University Press.

Zenger, Ursula
1973 "Die vier Sprachgruppen in der Bundesverwaltung." *Die Weltwoche*, Aug. 22.

Textbooks

Chevallaz, Georges-André
1974 *Histoire générale de 1789 à nos jours*. Lausanne: Editions Payot.

Grandjean, Henri, and Henri Jeanrenaud
1969 *Histoire de la Suisse*, vol. 2. Lausanne: Librairie Payot.

Hafner, Theodor
1969 *Kurze Welt- und Schweizer-Geschichte*. Einsiedeln: Benziger Verlag.

Halter, Eugen
1972 *Vom Strom der Zeiten*, vols. 1 and 2. St. Gallen: Fehr'sche Buchhandlung.

Jaggi, Arnold
1969 *Von den Anfängen der Reformation bis zur Gegenwart*. Bern: Verlag Paul Haupt.

Müller, Otto
1968, 1969 *Denkwürdige Vergangenheit*, vols. 1 and 2. Aarau: Kantonaler Lehrmittelverlag Aargau.

Pfulg, Gérard
1960 *Histoire de la Suisse*. Fribourg: Départements de l'Instruction Publique, Fribourg et Valais.

Pfulg, Gérard, Michel Salamin, and Maurice Zermatten
1974 *Histoire générale*. La Tour-de-Peilz: Editions Delta.

Rutsch, Walter
1966 *Welt- und Schweizergeschichte*, vol. 2. Zürich: Lehrmittelverlag des Kantons Zürich.

Weltgeschichte im Bild
1974-1978 Booklets 6/1-3; 7/1-3, 8, 9. Nordwestschweizerische Kommission für Geschichtsunterricht. Solothurn: Kantonaler Lehrmittelverlag Solothurn.

Index